The Long Walk Home
Matt Mattingly
Across the United States

by Buzz Eggleston, Editor, The Union Democrat, Sonora, California

When Matt Mattingly walked across America in 1990 he sent home weekly reports. The Union Democrat printed them along with a map showing his progress between New York City and the Golden Gate. But no amount of urging or badgering would get him to put the better anecdotal stuff into his reports.

After he got back he finally fessed up to why he was reticent to share the good stuff: "I'm saving it for my book," he said.

True to his word, he has saved the best stuff for last. *The Long Walk Home* is a good read, written with personality, humor, clarity, openness and an eye for detail. We travel each inch of Mattingly's 3,507 mile, 117-day journey and discover that wherever one lives, it is, in that person's view, "the most wonderful place in all the world."

We also learn that:

—Most Americans are remarkably helpful and giving, willing to share their homes with strangers and quick to provide a meal.

—Older men with backpacks frequently attract offers of rides from women, an astonishing percentage of whom are young and attractive.

—Americans treat their roadsides with disrespect. Mattingly counted 52,185 beer cans, 167,987 soft drink containers, 732 dead animals, myriad food wrappers, tires, cigarette packs, coins, keys, handtools, pens, caps, clothes and 2,142 disposable diapers, contents unexamined.

—There is, despite what they tell you, no flat road in America.

Most of Mattingly's book is warm and upbeat, but there are moments of sadness as when he arrives at his boyhood home in Colorado to find that all the friends he has wanted to see are still there—buried.

Two recurring themes in the book are the loneliness of the journey and his determination to finish what he had begun.

Finally, at the Golden Gate, there was a moment of dejection as he sat and looked at the great bridge. "The hoopla and foofooraw I had expected were not there. No one was there except Yvonne and I...no key to the city and no congratulations from anyone!"

But it passed. When Mattingly arose he reconciled himself: "I knew what I had done. I knew how much effort it took and I knew how I felt about it. I felt proud that I had done it and I was glad that it was over."

Mattingly's book, like his walk, is a personal achievement that rises above travelogue. He walked across America and, on the journey, he discovered much about himself.

To Jill
Enjoy Your
Adventure

THE LONG
WALK HOME

The story of my walk across the United States in 1990

Matt Mattingly

Monterey Pacific Publishing

ISBN 1-880710-38-2

Monterey Pacific Publishing

"While almost all of the names used in this book are true, a few have been changed where protection of privacy is appropriate."

Dedication

Dedicated to my wife, Yvonne, and her sister, Dorothy. Without their help this trip would not have happened. It is also dedicated to our three daughters, Karen, Doreen and Shirley. They often question the reason for my adventures but they always support them.

The last two hours of the long walk home were in San Francisco, eight miles from Sloat Boulevard and the Great Highway to the Golden Gate Bridge. My wife, Yvonne, joined me for the last two hours.

My mind was well above the highest clouds and I had trouble thinking of anything but finishing the walk. My pack felt light and my feet moved fast.

The night before I had called CNN, NBC, CBS and ABC. I had called the Mayor of San Francisco and the phone number I had for Police Escort. In every case when I called, I had talked to a machine and left the message that I would be at the Golden Gate Bridge at four p.m. I had been told there would be two or three vans of Kiwanians and several dignitaries to meet me. I was excited and exhilarated.

We arrived at the Golden Gate Bridge at three minutes past four on September 7th, 1990. The hoopla and the foofooraw I had expected was not there. No one was there except Yvonne and me. There was no cameraman to record the sight for television around the nation. There was no one to interview me about my long walk home and no photographer to take my picture for the morning paper. Not even any Kiwanians to discuss my ordeal or friends to share in my experience. No key to the city and no congratulations from anyone!

I sat for a moment and looked at the Golden Gate Bridge, a monument to the technical expertise of our society. I watched the tourists as they gawked at the bridge and photographed its beauty. My endeavor, my accomplishment was small in comparison to the magnificence of the bridge and the effort it took to build it, but the lack of anyone to share the trip with bothered me. This was not what I had led myself to expect.

After a minute or two of self pity, the scope of what I had accomplished came clear to me. I smiled to Yvonne, hugged her and said, "I did it. I walked from New York to San Francisco." She understood. I walked up to the bridge, wandered around for a while and then sat on the grass to admire the beauty of the bridge, the bay and the day.

*****

Four months and 3,705 miles back was New York City. Between the start and the finish were six pairs of shoes, a night with a gun-toting couple in Pennsylvania, a man in a motel in Missouri with a bathtub full of several bottles of whiskey, and a motel in Ohio which had identical keys to all the rooms.

On the trail behind me I could hear June saying, "I'll come and pick you up tonight. Your day of walking will only put you a half hour away by car."

The memory of the adrenaline rush when I was attacked by a brown snake and again when I faced an over-protective dog.

I recalled standing in a parking lot on a hot Kansas afternoon with a dozen people gawking at me because I was nude.

I could almost smell the cold mountain air as I crossed over the Rocky Mountains on Trail Ridge and the hail commenced.

A thousand memories were flashing through my mind. Most were good thoughts, but a few sad. The thoughts of Charlene, Herbie, Joe and Jimmy, friends my age that I had expected to see, but couldn't because they were buried before I arrived.

It had been a great experience and I was glad I had done it. I was also glad it was complete. I knew what I had done. I knew how much effort it took and I knew how I felt about it.

That no one was here to greet me didn't matter now. I took the trip for me. My wife was there to say I love you so the walk from New York to San Francisco was worthwhile. It was a good walk.

The Beginning

The Beginning

A few years ago I was in a bookstore with my daughter, Doreen. She casually asked, "Have you ever read Persig?"

"No," I replied indifferently.

She handed me a copy of Zen and the Art of Motorcycle Maintenance. A few days later I was immersed in Persig. I was not a motorcyclist and never intended to be, but this book got me involved in the longest walk I would ever take, a walk across the United States. Early in the book Persig talked about seeing the United States and he suggested that from an automobile there was a frame around all that you saw and this frame limited your ability to see the United States. Persig believed that a 'bike' was best. As a boy it took me two years to learn to ride a bicycle. I did not plan to ride a 'bike' across the United States. I decided that the best way for me to see the United States was to walk. It was this small seed, combined with my enjoyment of walking, that developed into my decision to walk across the United States.

I considered various walking ideas. I had previously walked the John Muir Trail and was considering the Pacific Crest Trail. The John Muir Trail was 211 miles and the PCT was over 2800 miles. The PCT would be a challenge, but it was commonly done and 2800 miles of trail was just 211 miles done fourteen times, fourteen hard times.

Then I remembered Persig and thought about walking on roads. Somehow my thinking developed into a walk across the entire country. Like most of my ideas, it sat there and developed slowly.

I kept putting the walk off one year to the next and probably would never have done it. One day I calmly mentioned it to a Bud Vogel who worked for the local newspaper, The Union Democrat. A few weeks later, at a social event, Bud introduced me to Harvey McGee, the owner of The Union Democrat. Bud calmly mentioned my walk and a few days later a young enthusiastic reporter came into my bookstore and said she would like to interview me about my walk across the United States.

I panicked. It was one thing for me to talk about it, but quite another to put it in the paper. As long as I was just talking about it, I could just keep right on talking about it. Procrastination! An article in the local paper would include times and dates, itinerary and places. If that happened I could no longer procrastinate. I told the reporter that I would call her in a few days about the interview, but I was not ready right now. Procrastination!

I took a few days off, hiked into the high country by myself and thought about the walk. Could I really do it? Was I too old at 59 to do it? How could I organize it? Where would I sleep? Should I walk on roads? Could I get support from some organization? Could I really do it?

I decided that I could indeed do it, but I should do it now at fifty-nine, before I got too old. Walking more than 3500 miles would be hard, physically hard, and require an absolutely firm commitment, but I knew that I could do it.

At home I talked it over with my wife, Yvonne. She did not give the walk her enthusiastic support, but she said she understood, and would give me her help. I guess after thirty-two years of marriage, a relationship that understands was probably the best relationship possible.

I called the reporter back and a few weeks later she wrote an article that captured the basic feeling I had of my walk. Her article gave me the enthusiasm to get in shape and to get ready for my long walk

If I was going to invest this much effort it should be for something other than my own self deification. Recognizing that the year I took my walk was 1990, I called the State Department in San Francisco. I suggested that if they could find a Russian to walk across the United States with me this year, next year we could walk across Russia, well, part way across Russia. They said that this was a poor idea, they would look into it and they would call me back. They never did.

Then I called the local Girl Scouts. We have three daughters. We were very active in Girl Scouts and it was a cause that I could support. They said they would get back to me. They never did.

One day I received a call from the Kiwanis International Foundation in Indianapolis. They interviewed me over the phone and printed a very good article in the Kiwanis Foundation newsletter about my intended trip. They asked if I would spread the word about the Kiwanis program, "Know To Say No." The program was a youth educational program about drugs and their detrimental effects. I enthusiastically accepted. This would be my banner. I have been in various Kiwanis Clubs for the last ten years so this was a natural.

The Kiwanis Foundation also pointed out that I would be near St. Louis in June when Kiwanis was having its International Convention. I had not planned it that way, but I checked and it was true. So the Kiwanis Convention was added to my commitments. Now I had a reason for my walk and I had a network of people to help

I wrote letters to selected Kiwanis Clubs located about a week to ten days apart, two hundred to three hundred miles apart. In the letter I included a copy of the article explaining the walk and asked them for some help. First I asked them to suggest the best route from their city to my next location about two hundred to three hundred miles further. I also asked if they could possibly house me for the night.

My letters must have been poorly written because I only received one reply. Chillicothe, Ohio, responded positively and the response was almost immediate. Since I badly needed someone at the start I wrote again to the Kiwanis Club in Union, New Jersey. They answered and suggested that the idea of walking through Newark should be reconsidered. I reconsidered.

At the age of fifty-nine I knew I had to get into shape for a long arduous walk. We lived ten miles from town so I walked to work three days a week. Since I owned Sonora Used Books, I had a sign on my pack, "If you read, honk. Sonora Used Books." I lost ten pounds in the two months before my walk. I was now in shape.

A few weeks before leaving on my walk a Kiwanis Club in New York City contacted me and offered help on my first day. This gave me confidence. I was ready

One last problem was the money. I had estimated that it would cost about $3,000 to take the trip. That would include meals, motels about a third of the time and various other expenses. I had about three hundred dollars saved for hard times. This bought my ticket to New York. We had a Visa with a $3500 limit that I took to cover my other expenses. I got a $500 advance in traveler's checks, stuck the card in my wallet and was ready.

My plans were settled. I would fly to Kennedy Airport on Sunday, May 13, and start my walk on May 14 from lower Manhattan, where I could see the Statue of Liberty. I would then walk west for 3,500 miles until I could see the Golden Gate Bridge. I would pass through Cincinnati, Ohio, where I had my first year of college. I would stop in St. Louis, Missouri, for the Kiwanis Convention. My mother was born in Savonburg, Kansas, some ninety years ago and I wanted to see her birthplace. From Savonburg to Denver, Colorado, where I graduated from high school, to Craig, Colorado, where I was born. My sister, Jo, lived in Grand Junction, Colorado, so that was essential. From Grand Junction to Sonora there was only one realistic route, through Las Vegas. I did not want to walk across the Great Salt Flats just east of Salt Lake City for that would mean four to five days of no water, no place to sleep, and a lot of heat. To go through Ely, Nevada, would require a three day supply of water on either side of Ely. I didn't have this requirement satisfied.

With the route determined, I was ready and eager to start. My schedule was simple. I had to complete the walk and arrive in San Francisco on September 7. September 8 would be our thirty-third wedding anniversary, and any wife who would let her husband go off across the country for four months deserved to have him back on their anniversary.

*****

I made a list of the items I would need to take with me. I added some things and dropped others as I discussed my trip with friends, but the final list was the minimum I felt necessary:

Pack with sign—Borrowed pack with a great sign. I added a PVC frame with a sign "New York to San Francisco – 1990". The frame was attached so that it would hinge on the top. The Frame with the plastic sheet sign could swing over the top and cover my head. This would give me shelter from rain, bright sun and hailstones.

Sleeping bag and pad—Tied below my pack was my down sleeping bag and a two-inch foam pad. If I was going to sleep under the stars, I wanted to be comfortable.

Two cameras—Both cameras were the point and shoot type, one with black and white film for my scrapbook and the other with color slides for presentations.

Toilet paper—(No comment.)

Two pair glasses—One was my prescription glasses that I needed to read maps and menus. The other pair were dark glasses because I knew that not all black tops are black.

Tape recorder and audio cassettes—To record my thoughts for posterity since I was a lousy note maker. Besides, I could record while I walked. The recorder used regular cassettes that I could buy along the way. Once I completed a tape I would mail it home.

Water container—1 quart. A cool drink would be welcomed on the road.

First aid kit—Including Advil, Tylenol and aspirin for my aches and pains, Neosporin and band aids for minor cuts and bruises, aloe for my tender skin, and two ace bandages for a possible turned ankle.

Emergency supplies—Blanket and lighter. The emergency blanket was light and small and the lighter was much better than matches.

Utensils—Metal cup for drinking along the road and my camping spoon and fork for eating. I had a Swiss Army pocket knife, with corkscrew, screwdriver and toothpick.

Flashlight—It would get dark and I might get lost so this would help me find my way.

Compass—So I wouldn't be lost as easily and when I did get lost at least I would know which direction I was going.

Water filter—A light straw-like filter in case I had to drink dirty water.

Hygiene necessities—Soap in container so I could look nice, toothbrush, tooth paste and dental floss to keep my teeth well, and my electric razor with charger so I would look well groomed. I have never felt comfortable with a beard. I also took some aftershave lotion so I would have a fresh odor.

Clothing—Handkerchiefs, two big red ones because I blow hard and often, a small light towel to dry my face and hands, 8 pair of sox, 4 pair of under-shorts. It would be important that I find someplace to wash my clothes occasionally. I took two pair of walking shorts and two Kiwanis 'Operation KNOW' tee shirts for wearing most of the time. One I would wear during the day and the other in the evenings. One pair of pajamas; if I stayed in a home, I wanted to appear civilized. I had my Levi 501's for comfort and durability, a long sleeve shirt for cool days, a Kiwanis jacket and hat to display my Kiwanis colors.

Shoes—Before I left I broke in four pair of shoes. I had a Podiatrist in Visalia who recommended Rockport shoes. I purchased a pair and found them very satisfactory so I wrote to Rockport and told them what I was doing, sent them a newspaper clipping and asked if, when I returned, they would consider me to promote Rockport shoes. They sent me a letter, wished me good luck and included a tee shirt and a pair of socks. My four pairs of shoes were one pair each of Rockport, Vasque, S.A.S. and Hi Tech. I planned to take two pair of shoes with me, the Rockports and one of the others, and have the other two sent to me when I needed them.

Feet support—2 pair of arch supports, moccasins for the evenings to relax my feet in soft warm comfort, a pumice stone to remove calluses and a large container of foot powder.

Food—Trail mix to eat on the road. Maybe it should be called "road mix." Instant breakfast that had lots of sugar and vitamins for instant energy.

Gortex jacket, trousers and hood—There was the possibility of rain, so I would be prepared.

Gloves—On cool mornings these would keep my fingers warm.

Tube tent with rope—If I was going to sleep out, I needed some cover, and this would be the lightest thing possible.

Map of New York and New Jersey—To keep me from being lost.

Envelopes—With my home address already on most of them. This would make it easier to write home.

Books—The three paperback books I carried with me were: Bach, Illusions; Tolstoy, War and Peace: Steinbeck, Travels with Charlie.

Garbage bags—One to cover my pack and one to cover my sleeping bag in the rain.

Newspaper articles about my trip to give to friends along the road.

Business cards that were really book marks, but they had my name and address on them.

Kiwanis Directory—I just took the pages that listed the names of Kiwanis Clubs in the states where I would be walking. This would help me with contacts.

Kiwanis "Operation KNOW" head band—To keep the sweat off on hot days and to promote the program.

Hip pack—I didn't know why they call it a hip pack when I would be wearing it on my stomach. Would "Tummy Pack" be better?

Note pad—To put down significant information.

Name pad—For the names of the people I met.

Address book—For important addresses.

Pencil and pen—To help with the items above.

Mace—You never know !!!

Airline ticket—From San Francisco to New York.

Money—All in traveler's checks.

MasterCard—For instant cash, meals and motels

Blue Cross card—In case I needed it.

AAA card—A gift from the Sonora Kiwanas for roadside help. Also useful to get maps.

Clippers—To keep my nails clipped.

Watch—I guess I needed to know what time it was.

I had checked and rechecked every item. I was ready to begin my walk

California to New York City

California to New York City

Yvonne and I left Sonora to go to San Francisco very early on Mother's Day, May 13, 1990. The distance from Sonora to San Francisco is about 150 miles. My plane was leaving at 10:30 a.m. from San Francisco International, but we arrived well before 8:00. Overcompensation, I guess. I got out at the curb, kissed Yvonne good-bye, took the pack from the trunk and hoped for the best. I don't like good-byes and Yvonne understood, so she smiled, shook her head and drove away. At least she would have some 'quiet time' on Mother's Day.

I was nervous, jittery and alone in a crowded terminal. It was too late now to change my mind, too late to postpone my walk. I had started my trip. Good-bye procrastination. This should have been the fun part, but instead it was just something that had to be done before I could really start my walk.

The flight to New York was more lonely than many of the roads I later would be walking. I was wearing my Levis and a long sleeve work shirt; most of the other men were in suits or sports coats with ties. The women dressed in suits or wool dresses. Many of the passengers carried attaché cases or portable computers. I had a fanny pack. We had little in common.

I arrived at Kennedy International on time at 10:30 p.m. Eastern Daylight Time. I expected the Kiwanis Club I had talked with in New York to have someone to meet me, but there was no one there. I called the local Kiwanis president, but only talked to his answering machine.

New York City and New Jersey

New York City and New Jersey

This was my first night, and nowhere to go. I considered getting a cab. I did not because I did not trust cab drivers. Twice in my youth, as a sailor, cab drivers had taken advantage of my wallet. I wasn't sure where I would end up if I asked a cab driver to take me to a low priced hotel, and I wasn't sure how low a low priced hotel would be. I knew the cab would be expensive. With a limited budget, I preferred the floor at the terminal. I finally took my sleeping pad from the pack, put my pack on the floor beside me and slept until dawn at the side of the luggage carousel.

Shortly after eight on Monday morning I called the president of the local Kiwanis Club again. Though it was obviously inconvenient, he came out to the terminal to pick me up in his plumbing van.

He smiled as he got out of his truck His smile was very sincere, the smile of someone who enjoyed what he was doing. He said, "I expected a much younger man." He extended his hand and we shook. Conrad had a firm handshake. I liked Conrad immediately.

"When I was younger I was working," I responded. "Like you," I added.

"I got your message when we got home late last night. It was too late for us to do anything. Where did you spend the night?"

"I slept by the luggage carousel."

Conrad responded, "I wish I had known, we could..."

I interrupted, "It was no problem. I slept well. I just don't know New York so I decided to wait until this morning to venture out." I could see he was bothered by my sleeping at the airport.

I continued, "I am trying to conserve cash, so the airport seemed best. I am no worse for the night. I expect there will be lots worse nights to come. Thank you for coming out to pick me up and get me to the city."

He drove me to his office, Billharz Plumbing, in Queens. Conrad was obviously a businessman. His truck was neat and arranged very orderly

The PVC additions I had made to my pack were beginning to come apart so he helped me glue the them together again. Both Conrad and his wife, Anne, were very friendly and helpful to me. Anne was effervescent and enthusiastic. She was apparently the bookkeeper, but it was obvious she was a lot more. I think she really ran the office, though Conrad wouldn't admit it.

They bought my lunch at local pub where two other Kiwanians

joined us. All four of them were active in the their Kiwanis Club and we discussed the various activities of our Clubs. Finally the president took me down to the subway station, bought me a token and sent me on my way.

I took the subway down to the World Trade Center. This was the first time I had ever ridden on the New York Subway. The graffiti at every station was extensive. A lot of it was meaningless to me, but I was certain it was important to the one who took the time to put it there. Some of the graffiti was very pleasing to the eye with complimentary colors and artistic shapes. It looked better than some of the ugly grays and browns it was covering.

It was about two in the afternoon when I got on the subway. Even though it was crowded, there were three people sleeping on seats in my car. They ignored the prodding and punching that a few inflicted in an attempt to get them to move to allow more seats. These were the homeless of New York. With my pack on my back I probably looked as I was just another homeless person, because none of the passengers would meet my eye.

I got off the subway and took a bus, another token, to Battery Park. From Battery Park I could see the Statue of Liberty. This was where I was to begin my walk. I decided not to take the boat ride out to the statue because the statue was a symbol to me, a symbol of what I hoped we believed. I was afraid that if I went out to the statue and looked at it closely, I would see that it was just a big piece of concrete and it would lose some of its symbolism.

As I was peering at the statue, a reporter from the New York Daily News approached me and asked about my trip. The reporter had an unkempt mustache which predominated his face. He talked very rapidly and I had to ask him to repeat many of his questions.

"Is that sign for real?" he asked point to my pack. The sign on the back of my pack, "New York to San Francisco – 1990" had garnered his interest.

I nodded, "That's my plan." It was difficult for me to say much more since I hadn't really walked any of the trip yet.

"How much does the pack weigh?" he asked, his note pad ready to record the information.

"Forty-five pounds," I responded. He looked as if he didn't believe me. He didn't write anything on his pad. I took the pack off and said, "Try it."

He did and found it was heavy. I wasn't sure how much it weighed, but I knew it was heavy. The reporter wrote something on his pad.

"Where are you going from here?"

"I plan to go up to the George Washington Bridge and cross over to New Jersey. Then I will walk west." I noticed he was writing everything down now.

We talked for another ten minutes and then he said, "I need some pictures." He directed me on where to stand and what to do. I think he was far more interested in taking pictures of my pack than he was in taking pictures of me. The pack, with the colorful sign, was far more photogenic than I was.

He took several pages of notes and a couple rolls of pictures, but to the best of my knowledge nothing was ever published. This was the first of many reporters who would interview me. I had never had many interactions with reporters before this trip. All the news people were exceptionally polite and trying to do their job. I enjoyed their company, and I hold them in high regard. I liked them.

About four o'clock I started walking north, intending on crossing the George Washington Bridge. I was not certain that I could get to the bridge or that I could even cross it. I asked one of New York City's Finest about the bridge.

He looked at me in amazement and said, "You can get to the bridge and you can cross the bridge, but do not."

"Why," I asked.

"Because you have to go through Harlem to get there," he replied. "You wouldn't stand a chance of walking through Harlem even if I walked next to you. Take a bus to New Jersey."

I thanked him for his advice.

A second police officer told me the same thing. I asked the second police officer what he would recommend. He suggested that I go back to California. I told him that was not realistic. He told me to take the bus over the river. He told me where I could get such a bus.

I did not want to be mugged the first day, or any other day for that matter. So I proceeded to walk to the Port Authority Bus Terminal on Forty-second Street and Eighth Avenue, to catch a bus to Union, New Jersey. On the way to the bus station I walked through some of the poorer parts of the city. At least to me they appeared poorer. The streets were dirty and it was not just recent filth, it was long-term filth. Many of the buildings had metal bars on their windows and all were dirty. The people on the streets never met my eye nor spoke to me. I did not feel comfortable.

I still did not have a place to stay that night in Union so I decided to call the one Kiwanian whose name I knew there. The call cost $2.25 and I didn't have that much change. Three different times I approached cab drivers sitting idly at the curb to get some change. Each time the driver asked if I wanted a ride. When I said, "No, I just need some change to make a call" they indicated their negative answer with the universal negative reply of the upheld middle finger. For the rest of my trip I never received that reply at any time for any reason in response to any request. From my days as a sailor I have been distrustful of cab drivers. New York City cab drivers did not change my attitude. On their side, within the past couple months several cab drivers had been killed and they were very cynical, but that still didn't warrant the use of the middle finger.

I finally got some change from a lady selling soft drinks on the street. When I called my Kiwanis contact in Union, I heard an answering machine tell me that his apartment had already been rented. I had no choice but to continue, so I headed for the bus station. I still didn't know where I was going to spend the night.

As I entered the bus terminal a young man asked if I knew where I was going, I guess I looked lost. He moved from one foot to the other very rapidly. It was a nervous habit I had never seen before. He offered to help me and he led me to where I bought my ticket to Union. There was some confusion because the first ticket they sold me was to Union City, not Union. When the young man directed me to the door to catch the bus he mentioned that I should pay him for his help. The only change I had at the time was a quarter, which I gave him, and told him I was too poor to afford expensive help. He smiled and moved back and forth on his feet quickly. With a distinct frown on his face, he shrugged his shoulders and wished me luck.

It turned out the door he sent me to was the wrong door and I had to come back to the information counter to find out the correct door. I wrote it down: Gate 222–Door 2–Bus 114. I am glad I wrote it down because it took me quite a while to find it. Once I got in line I asked the man in front of me if this is where I catch the bus to Union. He assured me it was. The bus finally arrived and everyone rushed aboard. I was carrying my pack and that made it difficult for me to maneuver down the narrow aisle. I found an aisle seat and stood my pack on my lap. Once the aisle was clear I tried to put my pack in the rack above the seats. My pack had to be pushed very hard. A young executive sitting across from me helped and we struggled but eventually shoved the pack in into the rack. We struck up a conversation and before we arrived at Union he had invited me to spend the night at his house.

Ken Rosengarten appeared to be all the things a young executive should be, tall, handsome, well educated, well dressed and able to carry on a conversation easily. He worked for an insurance company and was slowly climbing the company ladder. I felt he would have been happier in something more imaginative and creative than insurance actuaries. His wife, Evelyn, appeared to be very comfortable with the modern advancements in technology. She was finishing the work on her masters and was planning to continue her education in computers. She was very quick in her thinking and positive in her attitudes. They were a very enjoyable couple.

These two were in many ways very typical of the people I would meet in New Jersey and Pennsylvania. They took me in without any real knowledge of who I was or what I was. They fed me dinner that night and breakfast the next morning. They gave me a very comfortable bed with my own shower. In short they treated me great even though they had no idea of my background. This was to happen to me on many occasions in many places, all east of the Rocky Mountains.

Early the next morning Ken took me down to where he would catch his bus, just one block west of the center of Union. He gave me a couple of pins to show his enthusiasm for Penn State and sent me on my way down Morris Avenue, New Jersey Route 24. I was now on my way home.

I had the name of the president of the Kiwanis Club in Somerset so I called. He invited me to their meeting that evening. They met at a very fancy restaurant. Pete Johnson, a Kiwanian from the Somerset Kiwanis Club, invited me to spend the night at his house. I did and found it very enjoyable. The next morning he dropped me off on New Jersey Route 202.

This day, like yesterday, was rainy. I saw a large storm cloud heading toward me. The previous day I had been drenched even with my extensive rain gear. When I saw this storm coming I went behind a large road sign and changed to shorts and a T-shirt. I put a garbage bag over my pack and decided I could weather the storm.

The storm hit and it hit hard. I finally stopped and stood as far to the left side of the road as I could. The cars were only going about ten miles per hour in the heavy rain. I looked up and a New Jersey State Police Officer pulled up beside me on the shoulder. He rolled the window down on my side.

I knew I was getting old when he appeared to me to be a high school student, not a police officer. He had baby fat on his cheeks and I was certain he had not yet bought a razor. He yelled in a voice entirely too high, "I have been asked to inform you that there is a high probability of a thunderstorm."

I was standing in the middle of the heaviest rain storm I had seen in years and he tells me 'there is a high probability.' I laughed and said, "About a hundred percent."

He apologized for what he had said and asked me to get in out of the rain. I declined. I told him that he was heading in the wrong direction. He said he would go to the next turn around and get me on my way. I still declined. I told him I would get his car all wet and I explained that I was not suffering and that I would not melt.

He apologized again and went on his way. I am sure I know what had happened. A state police car I had seen earlier had probably called him, before the rain hit and said, "Someone ought to tell that old man there is a high probability of a rain storm." The young trooper did what he was told.

Pennsylvania

Pennsylvania

At 6:30 p.m. on Wednesday, May 16 I left New Jersey and entered Pennsylvania, ahead of schedule. The border between New Jersey and Pennsylvania is the Delaware River. I crossed this beautiful stream on a wide modern bridge. The stream was swollen for I could see trees along the edges with their trunks in the water. The gray water was moving quickly to the Atlantic Ocean only minutes away. There were no white caps, just the gray water undulating toward its destiny. I thought of the tune, "Ol' Man River." I knew it wasn't written about the Delaware, but the Delaware was a big river just moving along.

As I arrived on the Pennsylvania side of the bridge, I was informed by one of the toll takers that I could not walk across that particular bridge. I wondered if he expected me to walk back across his toll bridge. I didn't think so, but I wasn't sure. I asked him to take my picture in front of the toll booth and was met with a steely stare. He walked away and said to wait a few minutes. I thought he might call the state troopers, but instead another toll taker came. I apologized for having walked across his bridge. He explained that the rules were not his rules so he didn't care as long as no one was in danger.

He took my picture. Actually he did not take my picture because I found out several days later that my camera was not working, but he tried to take my picture. When I asked where I might find lodging he pointed down the road to New Hope. He also explained where I could cut across the grass of the toll authority to save myself some walking.

I did, and I arrived in New Hope only to find that the only hotel in town was too expensive, far too expensive. So I walked back to Lambertsville, New Jersey, on a bridge where walkers were allowed, and asked the police officer on the bridge where I might find a place to stay. He was not at all encouraging. We were discussing the alternatives available when from just below the bridge a man asked what the problem was. The police officer explained my problem and the man came up, identified himself as Jack Anderson and asked if I would like to sleep on his "party barge" for the night.

I said I was very interested. He tossed my pack on the hood of his pickup and drove me about a half mile downstream to his boat. His boat may not have been ideal, but it was more than sufficient. It was about twenty feet long and eight feet wide. There were two benches on either side and one in the stern where I could sleep. The sides of the boat were canvas, but they snapped down to keep out the weather. Jack said he lived in Lambertsville but the boat was his joy in life. Once

Jack felt that I was not going to hurt his craft he left. He explained that he had to leave for work before five the next morning and he had to get to bed.

I put my bag on the stern bench and soon fell sound asleep. During the night it rained, and rained and rained. Numerous whistles and sirens blew during the night to tell people the river was rising, and it did rise, almost five feet overnight.

During the night my bag got a little wet, but not sufficient to awaken me. In the morning I packed my bag, shaved quickly with my electric razor, and prepared for another day. I had some difficulty getting off the boat because of the high water. The moorings the night before extended up the side of the river about ten feet. This morning the lines were horizontal and it was about ten feet to the shore. I pulled on the stern line until I was close to shore. I tossed my pack on to the bank and quickly jumped ashore. I got a little water on my pants leg, but my feet were dry.

I walked into town, had a big breakfast of bacon and eggs at a small cafe in Lambertsville. My pack drew a lot of attention, but no comments were made to me. I set off again through New Hope and headed west on Route 202 through Pennsylvania.

On the morning of May 17, 1990, the beginning of my third day of walking, I was headed for Landsdale, Pennsylvania. My pack had not yet settled into place for the day so it seemed heavy. The rain from the previous night had put a sparkle in the trees along the side of the road. It would be a great day!

The greens of the trees, shrubs and grass were more than I had expected. I was basically a California person and California had green, but not like the green of Pennsylvania. I enjoyed the morning walking through Bucks County, Eastern Pennsylvania.

I will always remember Pennsylvania as being the most enjoyable of the states on my journey. It was spring and a very wet spring. I saw many shades of greens, deep dark greens, light yellow greens and every shade in between, greens that I had never seen in California. The roads I was on through Pennsylvania crossed several hills, went through many small towns and alongside numerous small streams. Of course I had to put up with a lot of rain, but it was worth it. It did bother me a little to know that back home in Sonora they were suffering from their fourth year of drought. I knew I couldn't change that so I enjoyed the spring in Pennsylvania.

It was along this stretch of road that I had an experience that was repeated, with variations, about two dozen times as I walked across the United States. A driver saw my pack and he quickly stopped and introduced himself as a traveling salesman. He asked several questions about my walk. How fast did I walk? When would I get home? How many shoes would it take? Why was I doing it? He explained that when he was younger he had ridden his motorcycle across the United States, but, he quickly said, "walking was different."

He asked if he could do something for me, give me some money, give me a ride, give me something to share in the adventure. I never accepted anything that would increase the probability of my being robbed. He suggested buying me a cup of coffee and anything else I wanted. There was a restaurant close by so I accepted his invitation. I felt it was very sincere and I enjoyed his company.

We talked for over half an hour as I enjoyed a blueberry muffin and three cups of coffee. He exclaimed several times how he would like to do something such as this, but he had to work to support his family, his two homes, his three cars, and his boat. I understood and felt sorry for him, for his life was like so many others I met. His life was not what he wanted, not what he had expected, but it was what he had to do because of so many obligations. He had slipped into obligations that he could not bypass. I felt better for the coffee and the muffin and set out on my walk again. Our conversation renewed my enthusiasm for my walk. I knew that my long walk home was also their vicarious adventure.

At about ten o'clock on that beautiful day, a blue van, going the same direction that I was, turned left onto a narrow side road about forty feet in front of me and stopped on the far side of the road. A very attractive woman with bright pleasing eyes rolled down the driver's window and asked about my venture. The sign on the back of my pack saying, "New York to San Francisco – 1990" had gained her attention. I explained that I was walking across our country. Within minutes she got out of the van and we talked for almost an hour. June was a free lance writer and she was hoping to get an assignment to write about my trip. I gave her all the help I could and promised to drop her a card in a few days. Before she pulled away I asked if she knew anyone in Landsdale where I could spend the night. She said she was sure she did and would check and she went merrily on her way.

Shortly before noon the blue van pulled up again. June appeared very enthusiastic. She explained that she couldn't find anyone in Landsdale where I could spend the night. "But," she added, "here's my phone number. When you get to Landsdale tonight, call me and I'll come to pick you up. You will only be a half hour away."

Ten to twelve hours of my walking at three to three and a half miles per hour was only the equivalent of about half hour of her driving in a car. This thought occurred to me several times as I crossed the United States, but it was never more evident than when she said, "You will only be a half hour away."

I called her that evening from New Britton and she came to pick me up. New Britton was short of my goal, but I had received three warnings from law officers that heavy thunderstorms were expected and there was a high probability of tornadoes. When the sky turned dark and lightning flashed across the clouds I decided it was time to end my day of walking.

This was the end of my third full day of walking and I hurt everywhere. At the end of my first day of walking I felt very good. I was convinced that this walk was going to be a breeze; I was in shape. At the end of the second day aboard the "party barge" on the Delaware River I was a little sore, but I didn't really hurt anywhere. Waiting to be picked up in New Britton, at the end of my third full day of walking, I hurt everywhere. The muscles on my legs were tight and they wouldn't loosen. My shoulders were stiff and sore and the top of my back hurt with every move I made. My feet had blisters and the middle toe on my left foot was swollen and bright red. I knew at that point that I was not in shape. I was very happy to see the blue van that evening, but very concerned about my ability to persevere for my long walk home. The evening with June, and her husband Karl, in New Hope, Pennsylvania, was a joy. They were just past fifty, their children were grown, and they had just applied to join the Peace Corps.

Their home was built in 1730. For an old man from California that was alarming. I knew that the history of California and therefore the history of the United States began in 1848 when Marshall found gold on the American River. General Lee of Revolutionary War fame had slept in this same house with his officers. On the hill across the road the enlisted men had camped. a soldier had died and was buried there. All the hills were covered with a deep green carpet of grass. It was a good place to live.

The next morning when I arose Karl had already left for his school bus run, but he left a poetry book open to Walt Whitman's poem, Song of the Open Road. June read the first and last verses to me and I was moved. Those two verses of Walt Whitman's poem became a part of my long walk home. I memorized them and often repeated them to myself.

I will always be thankful for my night in New Hope. It was a big part of my walk.

Song of the Open Road
by Walt Whitman

VERSE 1
Afoot and light hearted I take to the open road,
Healthy, free, the world before me,
The long brown path before me leading wherever I choose.
Henceforth I ask not good fortune, I myself am good fortune,
Henceforth I whimper no more, postpone no more, need nothing,
Done with the indoor complaints, libraries, querulous criticisms,
Strong and content I travel the open road.

VERSE 15
Allons! the road is before us!
It is safe - I have tried it - my own feet have tried it well
be not detained!
Let the paper remain on the desk unwritten,
and the book on the shelf unopen'd!
Let the tools remain in the workshop!
let the money remain unearn'd!
Let the school stand! mind not the cry of the teacher!
Let the preacher preach from his pulpit! let the lawyer plead with the
court, and the judge expound the law!
Comerado, I give you my hand!
I give you my love more precious than money,
I give you myself before preaching the law;
Will you give me yourself? will you come travel with me?
Shall we stick by each other as long as we live?

June drove me to the Landsdale Post Office early on Friday morning and I mailed some of my stuff home. My pack weighed forty-eight pounds when I arrived the night before. I decided I didn't really need several items in my pack such as pajamas, moccasins or the fancy Kiwanis jacket so my pack was now thirty-nine pounds.

The pain from the night before was subdued by Advil, there were few clouds in the sky and I was again headed west on my long walk home.

It was early on Friday morning that I had my encounter with a fast brown snake that attacked me. I knew there were no brown snakes in Pennsylvania and I knew that snakes do not attack but I was attacked by this big brown snake.

I was resting against my pack at the side of the road near Collegeville, watching the cars and feeling very sore and stiff. I realized I had rested too long. I slipped my arms into the straps while still sitting and pulled my pack forward and fastened the belt. I started to stand up. As I stood, a long brown snake came charging out of the grass. I saw it clearly and it was leaping at me. I turned to run. With my heavy pack and natural lack of manual skill, I tripped over my own feet and fell onto the gravel. I turned as I was falling and saw this long brown snake hit me in my right leg.

I winced, knowing it was going to hurt. When nothing happened I turned and saw that the long brown snake was just a piece of extension cord. The extension cord had caught on a piece of fishing line that had hooked on my strap. It didn't matter that the big brown snake was only an extension cord, I had panicked. I sat there for another fifteen minutes to let the adrenaline subside.

*****

Walking along the roads in Pennsylvania I was told there would be poison ivy. At our home in California we had poison oak, but I was told that poison ivy was different. It wasn't. There were several places where poison ivy was growing up next to the road and even across the shoulder. It was the same as poison oak. There may be a difference that cannot be seen with the naked eye, but it is small. I'm glad I knew what to look for from poison oak. I would hate to have been delayed with a bad rash.

Butterflies were often around on the walk. In Pennsylvania, near Phoenixville, I was taking a break at the side of a stream. I left my pack propped up by the road and walked down to the side of the stream for a drink. I relaxed and soaked my feet in the cool water. It was very pleasant and I stayed for nearly thirty minutes. When I returned to my pack, it was covered with beautiful butterflies, completely covered. I watched in amazement at such beautiful life. They were fragile and weak, for I knew I could crush them in my palm, but they were strong and hardy because their family had survived the cold winter.

They were constantly fluttering around my pack. Some would land and others would take off and flutter around. I tried to count them but there were well over two hundred. They were beautiful. They had small black and white spots on the outer edges of their transparent wings. The wings looked like tiffany glass with eight or ten panels that seemed very bright. The front of the wings were a translucent orange that seemed to extend beyond the rest of the wing. I knew there must have been something on my pack that attracted them, probably the salt from my sweating.

I wanted to get a picture of the butterflies, but my camera was in my pack. As I approached the pack, the butterflies would flutter away, so for several minutes I watched their beauty. Finally I got my camera, but the butterflies left, all but one. I did get a picture of my pack with one lonely butterfly. As soon as I took the picture, that one left also. I will always remember the beauty of those butterflies.

That evening I walked through Phoenixville. They were having some sort of celebration. A young girl explained that the festivity was for the horrid boys in Phoenixville. "They catch Frisbees in their mouth," she explained. I later found out that it was 'Dogwood Day.' I wondered if the young girl who I had talked with knew that a dogwood was a tree and not an animal. So much for the boys in Phoenixville.

Early the next morning I headed west. I walked through the very friendly town of Chester Springs. In Chester Springs a gray-haired lady with an old flowered dress stopped me. She said she had seen me yesterday on the other side of Phoenixville. She assured me that I was making good time and I should be in San Francisco before the snow fell. I didn't try to explain that it didn't snow in San Francisco but I told her I would be there well before winter. She handed me a bag of home-made cookies and gave me a big hug and a kiss on my cheek and wished me well. I thanked her very sincerely. I noticed the people in Chester Springs made eye contact with me as we met. Many of the people nodded and wished me good morning. I felt very comfortable there. It was a friendly town

*****

Around noon on the next day I was walking along a quiet road with wide gravel shoulders, only a few houses and very few cars. As I looked ahead I saw a large dark-colored dog come out from the side and look at me. Immediately the dog lowered her body and began a fast gait toward me. She didn't bark, but I knew she was mean. As she came closer I could see her teeth and hear a low growl.

I took out my can of spray to protect myself. When the dog was about five feet away I stopped and prepared to spray the dog. The dog stopped also. She was growling, curling her upper lip and baring her teeth. No amount of 'Good Doggie' was going to calm her down. I then made the mistake of establishing eye contact. As soon as I did she jumped toward me.

I had the can of spray in my hands. I wasn't sure if it would spray because I had never used it before. I wasn't sure that what they said was in the can was really there and I wasn't sure if I could use it.

But I did spray and the spray hit the dog in the nostrils. She merely glanced off my trousers and rubbed her nose in the gravel and grass at the side of the road. I walked on quickly, keeping an eye toward the dog. In less than a minute she again came toward me, but this time her tail was wagging back and forth as if to say, "You're the boss. You're the boss."

When I arrived at the place where she had entered she turned in and I was very relieved. I did wonder if her master noticed any change in her performance after our encounter, but I never went back to find out.

Later that same day I was on a very busy and narrow road. I had crossed a short bridge and decided to walk on the outside of the guard rail since the road was so narrow. Ahead I could see lots of activity and I was curious as to what was going on. There were lots of cars and people and animals running around. I was paying so much attention to the activity ahead that I didn't see a skunk just ahead of me. When I did notice the skunk, he was about five feet in front of me busily eating the remains of a McDonald Big Mac. The skunk noticed me about the same time.

I wasn't sure what to do. I knew if I tried to turn and run I would probably fall over myself, the snake had taught me that. I didn't want to use my spray because I knew I would be out-sprayed. I decided to back up slowly and hope that I wouldn't trip over something. As I moved the skunk gave me a dirty look, turned and walked into the bushes at the side of the road. I noticed the skunk left most of the Big Mac.

I was very happy the skunk was so understanding, but it took me a few minutes to get my mind straight and set out for the activity ahead. The big activity was a free dog-dip day at a local pet store. It must have been advertised well because there were lots of dogs there. The only real commotion occurred when a couple with a small cocker decided to reward their dog with some food. Several other dogs decided they should be rewarded also and there was lots of barking and snapping, but none of the canines or their owners were hurt.

*****

Early the next morning I again headed west on US 30. I had intended to stay south of Lancaster because I felt it was too large of a city, but I was advised to go through Lancaster, so I did. I was very disappointed. As I approached Lancaster I saw several horse-drawn buggies, the Amish. They did not stop to talk to me. They never even met my eye, so I never met any of them. I did notice that many of the rigs had electric turn signals and a rear reflector, for safety's sake I assume. I also admired both the horse and the buggy. They were beautiful, well maintained and a basic black.

As I walked into Lancaster, I saw a very large motel, obviously new. It had the shape of a show boat, complete with a neon paddle wheel and a calliope hooting away. I'm not sure what a showboat has to do with Lancaster since there was no river there or what it has to do with the Amish. It looked out of place. It also appeared very crowded, so I guess not everyone agreed with me.

As I walked through town there were several signs to get the tourist to come in, such as 'Authentic Amish Food', 'Visit Genuine Amish Farm' and 'See the Amish on their own Farm.' I had the feeling that the Amish people were the bait in a huge tourist trap. I was disappointed by this commercialization of the Amish, because I basically agree with the idea that we should examine some of our thoughts and actions and see if we can't get back to better beginnings. I was glad when I left Lancaster.

I saw a lot of squirrels also, both gray squirrels and ground squirrels. The cars noisily traveling down the roads did not seem to bother the squirrels as they chased each other about the fields or collected their food. But when I approached, they were very bothered. I was not part of the normal movement they had learned to live with.

Often when I took a break, I would sit so that I could view a field. The squirrels were industrious, always scurrying after something, looking for something or carrying something. They also watched the sky. As I was resting at the side of the road that afternoon in Pennsylvania, a large hawk was circling overhead. The squirrels still came out and collected whatever they were collecting, but they moved more cautiously. As the hawk came lower, several of the squirrels would find a hiding place, and the others moved only a small distance from their hiding places.

Finally, as the hawk came very low, all the animals would disappear from sight. As the hawk went back up, the squirrels would return. I watched the hawk fly higher and lower three times until finally the hawk left without lunch. I was glad. I liked hawks, but I liked squirrels better.

As I walked along the roads, I often disturbed squirrels and chipmunks along the side of the roads and they would chatter very loudly at me. I was not supposed to be there and they told me about it.

On a warm spring afternoon in Pennsylvania I was taking a break against a large oak tree when I saw two large gray squirrels a few feet away. I was eating some trail mix so I tossed them a few pieces. The squirrels liked the trail mix. After finishing the few pieces I tossed to them, they screeched for more.

Their screeching brought five other squirrels as well as several birds. I liked my trail mix and I knew I couldn't continue to feed them and me, so I merely watched as they argued among themselves for the crumbs and I enjoyed their screeching and scampering.

On the way to York I crossed the Susquehanna River at Wrightsville. I had seen big rivers before. The Delaware between New Jersey and Pennsylvania was good sized. I had seen the Sacramento River and the San Joaquin River in California and, years earlier, I had seen the Ohio and the Mississippi. When I saw the Susquehanna I was in awe. It was a mile and a half across that river at Wrightsville. I knew it was springtime and there was lots of rain, but the Susquehanna River was a big river.

*****

As I was leaving York the next morning a van passed me driving rather slowly. I saw it turn around and come back. The windows were dark so I couldn't see who was inside. Shortly the van passed me again and pulled into a driveway ahead. I pulled my can of spray from my tummy pack and was ready.

As I approached, the van window on my side rolled down and an attractive woman in her late twenties asked what I was doing. I quickly explained as I stood about ten feet from the van. We talked about the trip and I slowly approached the van. I could see another woman on the passenger's side. Between their questions they would talk to each other. The driver mentioned that they were going to San Francisco also.

I wasn't sure what they wanted, but the conversation seemed strange. There was no pattern to their questions. Finally the driver said, "We're driving to San Francisco. Would you like to come along with us? We're leaving tomorrow and we could share the driving. We'll be in California by Thursday."

I looked at the van, the smiling driver and considered the trip, but not for very long. I declined. If I arrived home two weeks into a four-month journey with two women, my wife would have some questions. This was more than just a walk across the United States, this was the adventure I always wanted. I knew there would be nights on this walk when I would regret not accepting their offer. I knew that in years to come, the walk would mean more than just a trip. I thanked them and continued up the road.

From York I went to Gettysburg and spent the night in a motel. Early the next morning I went to the Post Office in downtown Gettysburg and picked up my mail—my first mail call and a welcome one.

I felt better knowing that all was well at home. Yvonne said her work was doing fine. She was a loan officer at a bank and she enjoyed most of her work. Our dog, Lacey, was happy to have her complete attention. Actually Lacey was her dog, not our dog.

Karen, our oldest daughter, had sent me a letter explaining that her son, Kevin, missed me. I often thought of Kevin and what he would think of these sights, He was too young at four to really enjoy it though. Maybe in ten years. Karen said the baby she was carrying was doing well and would be born before my birthday, August 8. She said she was so big it had to be born before August.

My middle daughter, Doreen, was getting close to graduating from UCLA with her Master's Degree in Geography. I would miss her graduation and I felt badly about that. She told me she was very concerned about my being alone. Since she lived in Los Angeles, I could understand her concern.

Shirley, our baby daughter, was doing great. She was working as a waitress in Fresno, went to parties and was enjoying life. She said she was glad I was having such a great time. Everyone was doing great and Dorothy, my sister-in-law, was enjoying the bookstore. I mailed some items home to help lighten my pack.

The items I mailed were primarily things that had been offered to me along the trip. I had several business cards and menus with names. I also had some items I had picked up along the road. So far I had picked up thirty-three pennies, one quarter, one nickel, two wrenches, one empty money clip and the word "Friendly" from a license plate. I found and picked up more during my first ten days on the road than I did the rest of the trip. At the start of my trip I was tired, sore, and I kept my head down and looked at my feet more. This was because I hurt. My leg muscles pained me considerably and my feet had blisters and sores on almost every toe. My thoughts and my concerns were all within myself and about myself. During each day I was concerned about getting the pack right, setting my pace. I was worried about where I would spend the night and how far I would walk.

Once I was in shape, physically hardened to the walk, I found few things on the roads. They were still there, but I was looking up instead of down. My thoughts were of things outside my body: the road, the trees, the birds, the hills and the clouds in the sky, rather than the pains inside my body. If my pack didn't settle just right, it soon would. If my pace was not fast enough it didn't matter and where I would spend the night didn't matter either. Something or someone would work out for me. I often felt that my mind was outside my body too, a natural high.

Being high was something I had to watch. I didn't want to get too high, because the cars coming toward me at sixty miles an hour did not understand that my mind was outside my body.

Another mental problem I had was depression. I knew that nothing would end this walk quicker than depression. Since I was alone with my own thoughts all day long every day, I had to keep a positive mental attitude at all times. I nearly lost this positive attitude in Gettysburg.

I had planned to spend a day in Gettysburg. I wanted to see where Lincoln had delivered his address. I wanted to see where history had been made. When I set out to see the sights I was bothered by the advertising of the guides as "authentic" or "licensed" or "experienced" or "trained". I decided to walk around myself and see the sights and leave the guides to those more able to pay for them.

There were a large number of granite, marble, stone and wooden monuments to death, monuments to deaths that were unnecessary. I found myself with very negative thoughts. I threw the information about Gettysburg in a garbage can and left for Chambersburg. I could not allow depression to invade my thoughts. I planned to return to Gettysburg someday with my wife, and it will be very enjoyable then, but not now, not alone with my thoughts.

*****

As I was approaching Chambersburg, Pennsylvania, on a rainy night, a big brown Buick pulled up and stopped. The driver rolled down his window and offered me a ride. "I'm walking, thank you," was my reply. He said it was only a few miles into Chambersburg, but I said no. The driver shook his head and the big brown Buick slowly rolled away

When I got to Chambersburg, I found a cheap motel, showered and slept for about a half hour. I dressed and went out to find a place to eat.

I found a small 'greasy spoon' and entered. There were three booths and a long counter. I sat in one of the booths. I placed my order. About this time the man who had offered me a ride walked up to my table and asked if he could join me. I was glad to have company.

Then he looked at me and quietly but firmly said, "You really pissed me off this afternoon."

I am sure the surprise showed on my face.

"I could see what you were doing, walking across the United States. A great adventure. I wanted to share that adventure with you. A ride into town wouldn't have made that much difference."

I let him share. I let him buy my dinner. I decided that I had to rethink my 'walking' Would I accept rides? I knew that I wanted to enjoy my trip. I was not a purist and I was not making this walk to prove anything to anybody but me.

I decided that if I fell behind on my schedule, I would take a ride. A ride of three miles or five miles would give me a chance to meet another person, and a chance to rest for ten or fifteen minutes. Walking at three to three and a half miles per hour I could walk thirty to thirty-five miles a day, so in a hundred days I would walk 3000 to 3500 miles. But if something happened, good or bad and I stayed too long in one place, I would take a ride to get back on schedule. If I wanted to smell the flowers and watch the rivers flow, I would stop to do it. I was only going to walk across the United States once, so I was going to see and do as much as possible. I was too old to care about any record books and I wasn't going to worry about what others would think. I wanted to see the United States. I knew I couldn't see it all, but the part I did see, I wanted to enjoy.

After dinner we shared a bottle of red wine and I thanked him for being so honest with me. "Because of you I will accept more rides and undoubtedly enjoy my trip more."

*****

It rains a lot in the springtime in eastern United States. It had rained almost every day since I started my trip. Today was like all the other days, rainy, but it was also colder than usual. I was hoping to reach a small town near the Appalachian mountains, Fort Lauden, by nightfall. I was hoping there would be a motel in that small town, so I would not have to camp out in this rain.

Suddenly I saw someone in front of me. I looked up and there was a woman, smiling, standing in front of me. I calmly said, "Oh, an angel sent to carry my pack."

Smiling sincerely, she said, "Yes." She reached for my pack and I let her take it, all forty-five pounds of it. I could see a large blue van pulled to the side of the road with the door open. There was a man in the driver's seat and two boys in the back. I was happy to be out of the rain. They offered me a ride to town and I accepted.

After this long, cold and wet day I was eager to get off my feet and into a dry vehicle. I sat in the back with two curious boys staring at me. The driver introduced himself and his wife, Will and Kris, and their two boys, Pooky and Sooky. Within minutes they changed the invitation from a trip to town and replaced it with a night at their house with the understanding that I would have to listen to his political views. I gladly accepted.

Their huge home sat alone, surrounded by trees high on top of a mountain. There were numerous birds, squirrels and chipmunks all around. They showed me a bedroom and a bathroom and suggested that I soak for a while. I soaked in a hot tub. The only hot tub I found all the way across the United States. I felt guilty for so much pleasure after such hardship so I only soaked for a short time.

They asked me if I would like to join them for a ride into town to obtain some groceries. I agreed because I would see some of the country. I noticed that during this trip they both had hand guns tucked in holsters in their waistbands. I said nothing. I noticed that none of the clerks we encountered said anything either.

Politically, I have always considered my position being a little right of center, not very far right, but a little. Their position made me appear to the far left. They were born-again Christians, ultra right wing and very vocal about their beliefs.

They explained to me that the fall of the Berlin Wall was a communist plot to overtake the United States. "If Gorbachev didn't want it to come down, he would not have allowed it!" He believed that every "True American" should carry a weapon because "They" were going to get us if we didn't. Remember the year was 1990 and we were not yet out of the 'Cold War.'

During the evening, in their own house, they carried their guns. I asked, "Is this because there is a stranger in the house?"

"Does it bother you?"

I lied. I said, "No." I asked, "Why do you carry them?"

The reply was straightforward. "It is our constitutional right to bear arms." He explained that one evening some drunks were outside harassing them. They called the authorities but it took them forty minutes to respond. After that experience they had their phones removed. "They serve no purpose if they are not going to get us help."

They complained about the Supreme Court's decision regarding flag burning. I questioned which members of the Court opposed flag burning. I always felt that people complain without knowledge of the individuals who determine their future. They went through the entire Supreme Court, justice by justice, as to who had and had not voted and what their past history on voting had been. If Kris could not recall a certain justice's vote on a particular issue such as women's rights or abortion, Will did. They were intelligent, well-educated individuals with considerable knowledge of the world.

They appeared to mistrust others, yet they stopped to pick up an old man walking down the road on a cold wet evening. I always believed that people with a political position that significantly disagreed with mine were people who did not care, who did not really want to help. On my long walk home I found that political beliefs and caring were unrelated. This fine couple was indeed ultra-right wing, but they were also caring considerate people that I was glad to have met; I knew they would always respond if I ever needed them for any reason.

I slept well that night. Early the next morning we jumped into their van and they took me back to my walk. They gave me two big roast beef sandwiches, assured me I had God's blessing and sent me on my way.

*****

I found out that service station attendants do not know mileage figures, that is how far from here to there, or even what direction a place is. This was pointed out to me as I walked into Manns Choice, Pennsylvania. I had planned to spend the night in Manns Choice, but, I arrived there about noon. It was a good thing because there was no motel in Manns Choice. I asked the service station attendant how far it was to a motel. I was told, without any hesitation, that it was six miles up the road. He pointed the direction I was going.

I left Manns Choice happy as a dumb turkey in the middle of November. I walked for four hours and found no motel. As I approached a hill, I knew the motel would be at the top of the hill, but the hill turned out to be another two hours of walking. It was now about six o'clock and there was no motel in sight. As I walked past a graveyard, a young couple in a van were leaving. I asked the driver how far up the road to a motel. He said about twelve miles. I asked him if he had any water, because I was thirsty; I was also very frustrated.

The couple filled my water container and we talked briefly. Luckily they offered me a ride into Somerset. I had planned to go to Berlin. They pointed out that there was no motel in Berlin. I was very glad to accept the ride to Somerset where I found a Sleep Cheap Motel and a great restaurant, the Pine Grill.

The next day about five miles west of Somerset, I stopped at the top of a hill and was completely enveloped with a beautiful view. The hills for several miles could be seen, with a soft mist covering some and others displayed bright greens. At the bottom of the hill was a stream meandering among the trees and into a small pond. On the pond were a few birds and a doe and a fawn were on a far hill.

I rested for over an hour viewing that beautiful scene. I captured every detail in my mind for future viewing, knowing that later, long after my walk, when the world seemed too big to handle, this view would return, and the world would look a little brighter to me.

Sunday night I made it to Uniontown. The most amazing sign of my entire hike was on the road about seven miles east of Uniontown. The sign said 'DANGEROUS MOUNTAIN.' I took a picture of it, but it turned out that my camera was still not working so it didn't matter. I wondered how a mountain could be dangerous, and if it was, did it bite? Further signs explained that there was a six-mile steep downhill grade ahead.

It was on the road down this dangerous mountain that I knew my life was going to end very quickly. Walking on roads was significantly different from walking on trails. When walking on trails it was necessary to constantly watch where you put your feet. If you wanted to see the sights, you had to stop. If you tried to walk and view at the same time, you tripped and fell. Walking along the side of the road was different since the road was smooth and you could constantly look around and see the sights. It was like window shopping on a beautiful street called nature. If the shoulder was wide, your eyes and mind could meander well away from the road.

About half way down this 'dangerous mountain' I was moving very fast, wishing I could coast like a bicyclist. I was looking out across the large valley stretching out below and not watching the road at all. I had a ten foot shoulder so I felt very comfortable, and my mind was elsewhere.

The sudden loud blast of an air horn returned my thoughts to reality. When I looked ahead I saw a huge eighteen-wheeler coming up my shoulder. This monstrous truck was only fifteen or twenty feet away. I knew I was dead. I jumped to the side of the road and was going to go over the guard rail until I looked down and decided that was a bad idea; it was a couple hundred feet straight down. I pressed myself against the guard rail and the truck went on up the 'dangerous mountain.' I then realized that the monster was only moving about four miles an hour. If it had been necessary, I could have outrun it. I decided I should pay more attention to my road after that experience.

I entered Hopwood, a suburb of Uniontown, and was looking for a motel. I heard a noise behind me. I turned and there was an old man pulling a large black dog. He said, "You walk too fast."

I stopped and he led me to a bench nearby. He sat down, exhausted. He introduced himself as Joseph, "the Scarecrow of Hopwood". He was seventy-one and had the appearance of a very tired old man. His hair was unkempt and his clothes were too big for him. When I asked about a motel, he invited me to his house for the night.

He told me to remain on the bench and he would get his car and return. He took about fifteen minutes to return, fifteen minutes I enjoyed at the end of the day. His car was different. It was a big black 1974 Buick with the big engine. He had removed the front passenger seat so his dog could be more comfortable. I sat in the back and he and his dog sat in front as we drove to his house.

His house was completely cluttered from the kitchen, to the bedroom, to the bathroom. In the kitchen there were empty jars, dirty dishes, half-filled pans and several plastic containers on every counter and table. The bedroom was a mess with shirts, pants and shoes scattered around everywhere. He quickly cleared off the bed for me, tossing the clothes into a half-full closet. He showed me the bathroom which was full of his medicine containers, empty bottles of shampoo and tonic, and first aid articles long past any useful purpose. The shower was not real clean either. After I showered, he cleared a pile of books and notes from a chair in the living room and brought me dinner, heated canned peas and several pieces of KFC.

When I finished he put the dishes on the mantle and asked about Sonora. When I mentioned that gold mining was significant in the area, he grabbed his encyclopedia to see the weight of gold. His questions then wandered to lead, to Leadville, Colorado, to altitude, to altitude sickness and on into the night. He was lonely for conversation, but so was I. He was also curious. Next to his chair were three different encyclopedias and a set of classics. He constantly referred to his books as we talked to understand the world a little better. He was a fine person.

Early Monday morning he dropped me on Pennsylvania Route 21 headed for Waynesburg, Pennsylvania. I was two full weeks into my trip and beginning to feel great. My blisters were healing and my muscles were becoming hard. I felt very good as I headed west again.

The rain continued to come down as I approached Waynesburg so I stayed in the first motel I could find. Most of the night it rained and when I got up the next morning it was still raining. The clerk at the motel told me that it was expected to become clear by noon so I delayed my start until about ten. I had my pack covered so I headed out hoping for clear skies. Instead it just rained and rained and I was getting wet. It rained very hard as I walked through Rogersville but I headed down the road to Holbrook. I stopped at a small roadside mini-mart that had just opened. They had hot dogs, RC Cola and a few candy bars. I had one of each and ate slowly, hoping the rain would stop. I knew I was not in the city when I asked to use the rest room. They had one 'three-seater.' It had been forty-five years since I had used an outhouse, but suddenly, with one whiff, it all came back to me. Get it done fast and get out. I did, and I headed on down the road toward West Virginia.

West Virginia

West Virginia

I came to another store that was bigger and had more food. I stopped to rest and get out of the rain again, because I was soaked. This store also had a large warm stove, a bench close to the stove, and an owner who enjoyed talking. It was also Tuesday evening and my weekly report to The Union Democrat was due, so I called in my article. When the editor in Sonora, asked me where I was, I asked Gerald the store owner. He said I was in Nettle Hill. When editor asked the population, Gerald replied, "Three." I knew I was in the backwoods.

The people I talked with here were the same as the people in any other town across the United States. Their concerns were the same concerns as those in New York City, Somersville, Lancaster and Gettysburg. They all watched television, they all had children and they all wanted to live a happier life. Maybe I was in the backwoods, but the people I met were the same as the people I had met all along the way, sincere and caring, concerned and interested.

My rules on where I spent the nights were very simple. First choice, if someone invited me in, I accepted. Second choice was a cheap motel, that is, thirty dollars or less. Third choice was to sleep under a tree out of the sight of everyone. I carried a small tube tent and a down bag, so sleeping out was acceptable.

On a very wet night walking through West Virginia I arrived at a motel in Hundred at about eight o'clock. The rain was coming down in torrents and I needed a warm dry night's rest. The clerk turned on the 'No Vacancy' sign just as I opened the office door. I quickly asked if he had any place for me to stay that night.

He was not happy with me. I was a transient, it was late and he wanted to watch television. I smiled and he stared at me. After a two minute stare-down he decided that I wasn't too bad. He said he was just closing but he said he had one room left. He told me it would be twelve dollars, cash, no plastic. I gave him twelve dollars. He gave me a key and directed me to a small cabin at the end of a row of about five small cabins.

The room was very small, damp and musty, but I did not see any water dripping from the ceiling. I took a quick shower using water that I am certain would not meet any standards, anywhere. I ate three Twinkies from my pack and took two Advils for my aching body. I pulled the string to shut off the lone light and lay down.

Just as I was about to drift off to sleep, I remembered that I had not filled my plastic bottle with water. With heavy activity during the day, I would wake up at night very thirsty, so I kept water by my bed.

I reached up and pulled the string and turned on the light. I saw at least five hundred little six-legged creatures running all around the ceiling, walls and floor. I wanted to leave immediately, but I didn't. There was no place to go. It was dry inside and very wet outside. I was tired and needed a rest. I took the water bottle from my pack, filled it and made sure the lid was on tight. I shut off the light and finally fell asleep.

*****

The next morning the sun was shining and I was glad to be a part of the world. I had another odd animal encounter as I walked along a road in West Virginia. It was a bleak and sullen day with an occasional light shower. I had been on the road for a couple of hours. I noticed a turtle starting to cross the road in front of me. I had seen several squashed turtles on the road. Recognizing this turtle would probably be squashed, I picked him up and put him back in the bushes.

As I started to walk on, I heard someone call out to me. I looked and saw three farmers at the side of a field, leaning on their hoes. It was too wet for them to work the field, so they just leaned on their hoes. When I approached, one of the hoe-leaners said, "Won't do no good."

I was confused. He said, "The turtle. It won't do no good to put it back because it has iron 'maggots' in its head and it will just go across again."

I contemplated his idea of 'iron maggots' and nodded.

"Looks like it's a gonna clear up," one hoe-leaner said.

The second hoe-leaner shook his head. "Not today it's not," he said.

The first hoe-leaner stooped and picked up a jug from between his feet. He raised the jug with his elbow and took several gulps. He looked to his two companions and they shook their heads. He turned to me and asked, "Care for a drink?"

I had visions of a back woods still, corn liquor, and the revenue agents coming down the road. "What is it," I asked.

"Best tasting stuff you'll ever know," he replied.

I didn't consider his reply a challenge, but I was curious. I took the jug, raised it just as he had done. He was right. It was root beer, and it was good. We talked for a few minutes about the rain and the mud. He offered me another drink and I accepted and then departed on my road.

The next time I saw a turtle crossing the road, I carried it to the other side. I did not believe in iron 'maggots' but the idea that instinct told the turtle which direction to go was probably correct. I also imagined the taste of that home made root beer again.

They told me in Hundred there were three hills leading down to the Ohio River. That was true, but they sure seemed like large hills. As I was walking down the third hill I looked ahead and saw a large river. It didn't occur to me that it was the Ohio River. At the top of the next rise I looked again. It was the Ohio and I let out a loud yell. In my mind I had decided that if I could reach the Ohio River, I could cross the United States. I was approaching the Ohio. I enjoyed a glass of red wine that night in New Martinsville, West Virginia, on the bank of the Ohio River.

*****

I left New Martinsville after mailing another package home and discovered that walking south on West Virginia Route 2, on the east bank of the Ohio River, was difficult. The shoulders were very narrow and in many places non-existent. The saving part of walking on this road was that the traffic was not very heavy. When vehicles came, I had to stop and step aside. This slowed my pace considerably.

I noticed most of the towns I went through along the Ohio River were not prosperous. The decreased steel production and the associated industries hurt them. There were a lot of 'For Sale', 'Available' and 'For Rent' signs, and several empty houses and vacant retail stores.

Yet there was still a lot of industry. I saw several trains loaded with coal. These trains were about 180 cars long and they moved very slowly, about fifteen miles per hour. Apparently most of the coal was going to power plants. There was very little river traffic, but it was springtime and the Ohio River was higher than usual. Since it was higher, it moved faster and that meant more power and more time to move the barges upstream.

In St. Marys, West Virginia, the Kiwanis Club honored me with a great motel room. After a shower I walked around St. Marys to see the sights. The primary sight to me was the Ohio River. I was still elated that I had come so far, was feeling great, and was still on schedule.

The people of this country were great to me. As I walked around St. Marys, I stopped at the local drug store, Phillips Pharmacy, to get some film and arch supports; my feet felt better, but they still needed help. The owner of the pharmacy, Chuck, offered me a cup of coffee, which I gladly accepted. We talked for a while and as I left I asked him to direct me to the best place to have supper and a glass of red wine. Chuck suggested the Fireside Restaurant and Lounge, and even told me which door to go through, the one that said 'AACB Members Only.' I told him I was not an AACB member. I didn't even know what it was. He waved off the comment and asked me to trust him.

I assured him I would and I thanked him and walked around town a bit more. St. Marys had cleaner streets, better kept buildings and fewer for rent signs than any of the other West Virginia towns I had walked through.

Finally I went into the Fireside Restaurant through the prescribed door. Inside were a comfortable bar and restaurant. The waitress asked, "Is your name Matt?"

I was very surprised, but I said it was and she told me that the owner of the pharmacy had called and said that tonight my drinks and food were his treat. I had two glasses of red California Burgundy and some fine barbecued ribs. I slept very well that night.

Ohio

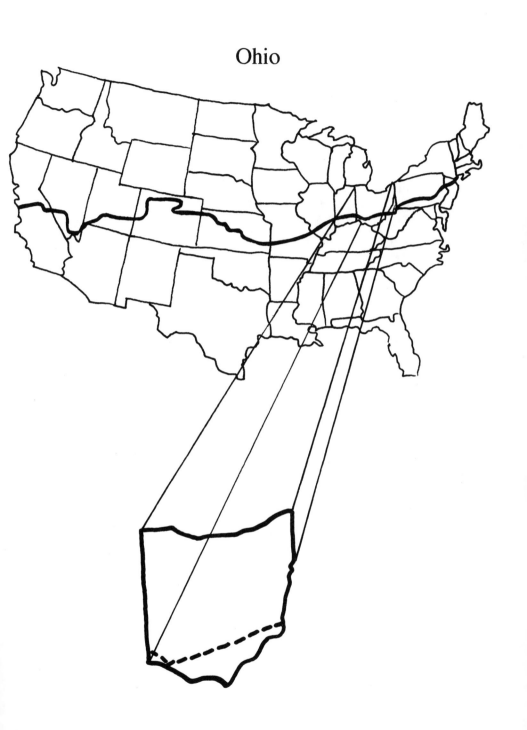

Ohio

Early the next morning a Kiwanian took me across the Ohio River and deposited me in the state of Ohio on Route 7. It was June first and I was feeling exceptionally good that morning. Just before lunch a car pulled up and the driver identified himself as Bert. He said, "I was expecting you. Get in. We have an appointment with the mayor of Marietta."

I had lunch with the mayor of Marietta, and several others. A local radio station interviewed me during lunch. After lunch there was a lot of picture taking. They made me feel like royalty. Once Bert took me back to my walking, the reality of walking replaced the fantasy of royalty.

The next motel I stayed in cost sixteen dollars, cash. It was late evening when I got to my room. I showered, and then laid down on the bed to rest. I immediately fell asleep.

I awoke when I heard someone rattling the knob of the door. I remembered that I had locked it, so I was not worried. The lock turned and a young woman started to enter. She said, "I'm sorry."

For some dumb reason I also said, "I'm sorry." She quickly closed the door.

I dressed and went outside to see how this could have happened. Two couples were moving from Tennessee to Detroit and they had rooms on either side of me. I asked to see their keys, and I compared them to mine. They looked identical.

I went to the office and told them what I had found. They confirmed that the keys were identical and explained that it was much easier to keep track of keys that way. "Besides," she told me, "we save lots of key expenses." I guess when you run a cheap motel, you have to conserve every way you can. This situation did not bother me. I had nothing that anyone would want to steal. I slept very well and awakened early the next morning, eager for another day.

*****

I saw several deer on the walk but the one that I remember best was near the top of a small hill just east of McArthur, Ohio. It was on a bright Sunday morning. A large doe came bounding down out of the woods, stopped in the middle of the road and peered at me. The deer I had seen so far were much larger than the deer I had seen in California. They appeared much more majestic.

I knew that this beautiful doe could be road-kill if she didn't move soon so I raised my arms and yelled at her, expecting her to turn and run.

Instead, she merely flicked her ears and took a few steps toward me. She stared at me for over thirty seconds and I stared back in amazement. After her thorough investigation she bounded back up the hill from where she had come, and disappeared into the woods.

She really made me feel good. I decided that she had come down out of the woods just to investigate me and wish me well on my walk. When she was satisfied, she returned.

*****

I passed a small stream near the junction of US 50 and Route 356 that had apparently flooded the road within the past few days. The mud from the stream bed had accumulated on the shoulders of the road and it was slippery. There had apparently been quite a windstorm also, because I saw several fallen trees that had their spring leaves now dying on broken branches. Nature had indeed been harsh here. I was told by several people that this was a very wet year for walking and that I should have planned my walk for last year. I listened, but I didn't believe. I've heard this same story about fishing. The fisherman who had nothing said, "Everyone caught their limit last week, you should have been here." The wind surfer sitting disgustedly on the shore said, "The wind was beautiful all last month, you should have been here." And when it got hot they said, "It's too hot today, but yesterday it was nice and cool."

I spent Sunday night in a small, old, cheap motel about two miles west of McArthur. Luckily I was carrying my food, because there was no restaurant close by. The roads in Ohio were enjoyable. Ohio has several roadside rests which are helpful to walkers. A chance to sit and rest with water and a bippie.

*****

On Monday I walked to Chillicothe where I received mail from home. I was glad to hear that all was well. I spent the night with Paul and Joyce Leach. Paul had responded way back in December to my plea for help. I went to the Chillicothe Kiwanis Club meeting on Tuesday noon and they sang a song to me, When Matt comes marching home again, Hurrah! Hurrah!

The Chillicothe Gazette came out to Paul's house to interview me as soon as I arrived. The reporter, Jane Schmucker, was the only reporter who insisted upon discovering my given name. No, it was not Matt or Matthew. It was Marvin, but I didn't like the name Marvin, so I insisted on being called Matt, exclusively. She also insisted on examining everything in my back pack. Since I attended the noon meeting of Kiwanis the next day, I was able to read the report before leaving. They misspelled Paul's name, but they got my name correct, including Marvin.

From Chillicothe I walked on US 50 to Hillsboro, where the creator of Steve Canyon was born. What importance to the world that was I didn't know. I had planned to stay farther north, but was told US 50 had bigger shoulders and less traffic. Wide shoulders and fewer cars were important to me so I walked on to Hillsboro.

The next day I headed toward Cincinnati on US 50. The previous day had been relatively clear, so many people had mowed their grass; the odor was very strong. There were also a lot of birds that time of day and their music was very enjoyable.

Shortly after seven in the morning I took a break and doctored my feet, as I often did. A van pulled up and the lady driving, whom I had met the previous evening, asked me to get in. She wore a simple cotton dress and her hair was pulled back in a pony tail. Her smile was tentative, but business-like. She wanted to take me back to Hillsboro for an interview at the Senior Center. I agreed if she would return me to where she picked me up. She said she would. I held the interview and afterward an elderly man offered to take me back to my route. He said he preferred the back roads because he didn't like the traffic lights on US 50. There was actually only one, but he didn't like it. He took me by where the train used to go and by the one-room schoolhouse where he went to school and he drove me by his old home, two miles from town. A lot of what he was raised with was important to him. As he dropped me off, back on US 50, he mentioned that this part of the country was one of the most beautiful anywhere. I agreed, and thanked him for the ride.

Along the roads of Pennsylvania and Ohio there were used car lots, complete with flags. Used car lots must have flags, preferably old tattered, plastic, multicolored and faded flags. There were used car lots in California, but along here the lots were out in the middle of nowhere, ten miles from town and nothing else around. I never saw anyone at the lots, either customer or salesman, but the lots were there. The only place in California that I had noticed an isolated used car lot was in Hughson, but everyone knew that Hughson was Hughson. I decided the car lots were fronts for husbands to convince their wives they were really working.

The motel I stayed in Cincinnati was one of the best, at least as far as I was concerned. I reached the town of Milford, on the outskirts of Cincinnati, and planned to stay there for the night, but there was no motel on US 50. I was eating at Big Boy and pondering what to do next.

As I finished my meal, a man stopped to talk with me about my walk. When I mentioned that there were no motels here, he offered to take me up the interstate to a motel.

He took me to the Red Roof Inn, about five miles north of US 50, and I went in to register. The clerk, a very young dark-haired girl, was very involved with a book. Since I own a book store in Sonora, I understand and appreciate individuals who are so consumed. She was very routine about her job. She pushed the sheet toward me and asked me to fill it out without looking up from her book. I filled out the form and returned it to her. When she read the form, she pushed it back and, without looking up, informed me that she had to have my automobile license number. I said I had no car. Again she insisted on my automobile license number, explaining that if she didn't have it, they would probably tow my car away during the night. She still had not even looked up from whatever she was reading. I didn't notice the title of the book, but it had a lot of cleavage on the cover. I assumed it was a historical romance.

I had my pack on my back, so I just waited for her to come to her senses. After she completed the paragraph she was reading, she looked up from her book. I told her I was walking and had no car. She did not believe me at all. She smiled very smugly and again told me to write down my automobile license number. I turned around so she could see the sign on the back of my pack, but she was not impressed.

She shook her shoulders and told me not to blame her when they towed my car away. I decided that she didn't understand, but I also decided it didn't matter to me. They were not going to tow my car. As I took the key and turned to the door it must have occurred to her that I was serious, because she asked me to wait a minute. She stepped outside and talked to the gardener. At least I thought it was the gardener since she was planting flowers in the front area.

She came in and introduced herself as the manager and asked about my trip. When I told her I was walking from New York to San Francisco she seemed very excited. We talked for a while about my trip, when and where I had started and when and where I planned to finish. Finally she turned to the clerk and informed her that my lodging would be complimentary. I thanked her profusely, because I had not expected it and I appreciated it. She also gave me a Red Roof tee shirt and I gave her a tee shirt from Tuolumne County. We talked for quite some time. She was very competent and enthusiastic about her job as manager.

Later that evening I went across the street to the Montgomery Inn. Because of my walk the Montgomery Inn treated me to my red wine and some of the best ribs in the world. I enjoyed my evening in Cincinnati, and I enjoyed the people there also.

The weather that evening was ferocious. I was told they were having tornado watches. I know that the wind was sure howling most of the night. The weather reports I received were generally second hand. That is, I asked people what the weather report was. I depended upon other people because even when I stayed in motels, I did not watch television or listen to the radio. This trip was MY trip, and no announcer or commentator was going to decide what I thought about. I did discover that weather reporters in western Pennsylvania and Ohio were phenomenally inaccurate. They were completely wrong.

I have always believed that if you predict tomorrow's weather to be similar to today's, you'll be more accurate than most weather prognosticators. My first night in Cincinnati was terrible. Not as bad as the tornadoes that were in Indiana, but still terrible with high winds and lots of rain. The next day I was told it would be clearing by mid-afternoon. Not so. It rained and stormed that night also.

The next morning there were tornado watches for the area. The wind was blowing wildly. Rain and occasionally hail was pelting the ground. I decided to take a day off and rest my weary bones.

Indiana

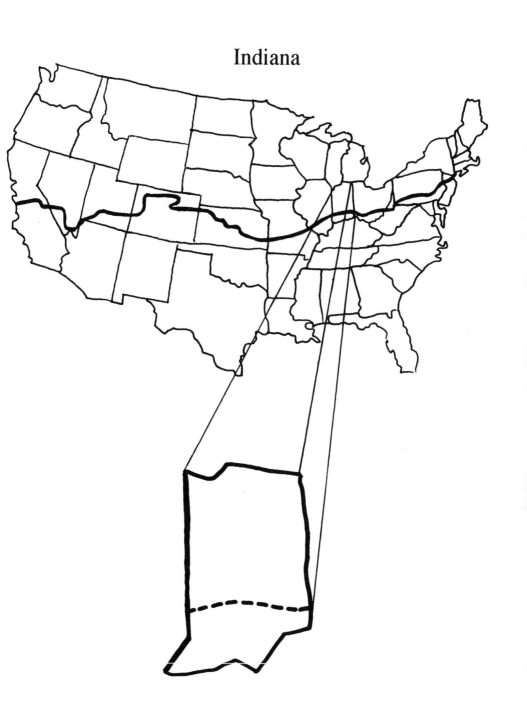

Indiana

Early Friday morning I entered Indiana to resume my walk. All was well for about fifteen minutes and then my legs began to cramp and my feet began to hurt terribly. I decided that a day off had spoiled my legs and feet. I slowed my pace considerably for about an hour and most of the pain went away. Perhaps the Tylenol helped. By noon I was back to feeling great and walking at about three and a half miles per hour.

In Indiana there were no berms. Berms were the same as shoulders, but in Indiana they called them berms. By ten o'clock the berms had widened and the walk was very enjoyable.

Before noon I saw one of those signs, that I disliked, 'CONSTRUCTION AHEAD.' That sign meant that any number of problems were just down the road. There were other signs that were very alarming also, such as, 'ROAD NARROWS AHEAD', which meant there were no shoulders at all. 'NARROW BRIDGE' meant that you were going to play Russian roulette with oncoming cars. Probably the worst sign was 'LOOSE GRAVEL' which meant that I had to try to dodge oncoming rocks or find another route. I usually chose the latter; I'm a poor rock dodger.

I also discovered that NASA helps the highway departments with the design of the rocks they use on highways. It was perfectly logical. Walking along the highway there were always small rocks. These rocks always had sharp points. As I walked the rocks would be tossed backwards, away from me. But, with the help of highly sophisticated aerodynamic engineers, the rocks would turn and come back toward me and drop into my shoe. Because of their sophisticated design they would immediately go to the bottom of my shoe. The sharp point of the rock would aim directly for the most tender spot on my foot and jam into my foot. I had to stop and remove this small but worrisome rock. When I looked at it, I could tell it was made to stick into my foot and make me stop. I was very impressed with the design of these rocks, but I discarded them into the roadway immediately. I decided to let the cars worry about their design, I had some walking to do.

A major problem I had was flat land or rather the lack of it. In Pennsylvania and in West Virginia I was told that Ohio would be flat. I found out that was not so. Several people in Ohio told me Indiana would be flat. I was now in Indiana and it was not flat, it was still very hilly. When I asked about the next state, Illinois, I was told that it would be flat. I tried hard to believe them.

Walking on the roads was not the same as driving. Hills meant nothing to a driver. To a walker each hill was almost a mountain. The pack became heavier and the pace slowed. Up a steep hill was bad. Flat was good. A little downhill was even better. A steep downhill was also bad. I looked forward to flat, which was just one state away.

*****

Another interesting night was in Versailles, Indiana. Versailles pronounced, in Indiana, to rhyme with 'rails.' As I came into Versailles it was getting dark. The first motel was filled and so was the second. There was a gathering of muzzle-loaders in the area and all the rooms were taken. Versailles had only two motels. The night was not a nice night to be outside so I wanted to sleep inside. I went to the ISP, Indiana State Police, which was next to the second motel.

Throughout my trip I was treated very well by state police, and in Versailles they treated me with full honors. The officer I talked with immediately called the Captain at his home. He came into the office at once, in shorts. Three people were trying to find this old man a room for the night.

Finally the Captain asked me if I had 'funds.' I assured him I had some, but limited. He told me he had a room for me at the local hotel, Room 6. One of the officers drove me to the hotel.

"Where do you call home?" the officer asked.

"Sonora, California." I replied. "Sonora is a small town in the Sierra Nevada Foothills. Near Yosemite National Park."

He shook his head and leaned over closer to me. "Since you are not from around here," he hesitated as if searching for the correct words to use in front of a stranger. "You should be aware that Versailles has a few," again he hesitated. "A few 'rednecks.' So be careful" He escorted me into the 'lobby' that was actually a bar, and asked the man behind the bar, "Is this the place where we have a room reserved?"

The man behind the bar told the trooper that this was the right place. The trooper grinned to me as he left. After looking around the bar I decided that a 'redneck' was anyone wearing dirty jeans, cowboy boots, and drinking Budweiser beer from a long-necked bottle. I was wearing shorts and low walking shoes. There were about ten Budweiser beer drinkers sitting at the bar and two booths with another six or seven Budweiser beer drinkers. All were wearing cowboy boots and dirty jeans. All were drinking their Budweiser from long-necked bottles, no glasses, thank you.

The man behind the bar grinned and informed me that it would be about fifteen minutes before Room 6 was available. One of the Budweiser beer drinkers in the booth closest to me asked, "How come you have such an elegant escort?" 'Elegant' was said with a definite sneer.

I looked at the young man who had questioned my escort. He had a tooth missing in front and an intimidating grin on his dirty face. He wore a baseball type hat, turned backward. It was too dirty to read what was written on it. Since I was expecting a 'redneck' harassment, I decided to take the offensive. "Because I'm so damn good looking." There was a hint of laughter from the bar, but not from my inquisitor. I turned to the man behind the bar and slowly asked, "Since I have to wait, could I please have a glass of good red wine, at room temperature?"

The hint of laughter turned to a loud snicker. The man behind the bar told me he had no red wine. When I suggested white wine, he just shook his head. My inquisitor suggested a Budweiser. I smiled and told him I had seen the horse on the side of town, so I knew where that beer came from. Even he laughed that time.

The man behind the bar invited me to see what drinks he had to offer. He had only three drinks in the entire bar; Budweiser beer, Jack Daniels and Jim Beam. He explained that no one ever ordered anything else so he had no reason to stock anything else. I thanked him for showing me his three offerings, but declined any drinks that evening. I was tempted to explain that if three kinds are all you offer, three kinds were all anyone would order.

A few minutes later an old man came in from the back and the man behind the bar asked him to show me to Room 6. Room 6 was a large room with some boxes stored on one side. "Just stuff," said the old man. He told me the bath was down the hall and he started to leave.

"May I have the key?" I asked

The old man looked surprised, shook his head slowly and said, "We don't have no keys. But don't worry, no one has ever lost anything. You'll be safe." I had to accept his word, there was nothing I could do about it and it probably was no worse than all the keys being identical.

Then I made a mistake. Since the room was stuffy I decided to open the window, the only window. I had to pull hard on it, but it did come open. But then I couldn't close it. Friday night in Versailles was very loud. Several drivers decided to see how long and how hard they could run their engines at full throttle. Quite a long time I discovered. They also attempted to see how much rubber they could burn leaving the parking lot. They burned several inches for several minutes. There was a group of drivers speeding their cars around the hotel and slamming on their brakes to see how far they could slide. All three activities, roaring engine, burning rubber at take-off and screaming to a stop, were going on simultaneously until almost one in the morning. As the noise quieted, sirens wailed into the lot below my window and there was a lot of yelling and screaming. It was a big Friday night in Versailles.

I rose early Saturday morning and left the hotel. I left without a shower, because I couldn't find a shower that wasn't caked in rust. The two showers I did find only had one faucet, cold water. Breakfast that morning did taste good, but Versailles, pronounced to rhyme with 'fails' in Indiana, was often in my thoughts afterward.

*****

The next stop was Seymour, a thriving, congenial town some thirty miles away. Often, before I reached a town, I was able to get some idea of the character of a town. About fifteen miles out of Seymour, a car stopped and the driver offered me a ride. The driver was a very attractive woman in her twenties, driving alone.

I declined the offer of a ride and explained that I was walking. She asked if I was going to Seymour. I said I was and she invited me to the Taco Bell in Seymour. She said she would buy my dinner. I told her I would be there, but it would be a while.

Six hours later, I called the President of the Seymour Kiwanis Club and explained that I had just entered Seymour. I asked if they might shelter me for the night, and explained that I was headed for Taco Bell where I had an invitation for dinner. The member I called wasn't real encouraging since he had to leave within minutes for a wedding, but he said he would call another member.

It was less than a half mile from the phone to Taco Bell, but a Kiwanian, Don, picked me up before I got there. We went to Taco Bell and the manager was happy to see me. She asked what I would like for dinner and I told her I had no idea. She selected the items and it was great. I seldom ate at fast food restaurants, but tonight, with such an invitation, I made an exception. Exceptions were permissible on such a long walk home.

When I finished, I thanked the manager for a fine and filling dinner and Don escorted me to a motel, paid for by the local Kiwanis. He informed me that breakfast the next morning at the Cracker Barrel next door was also paid a gratuity of the local Kiwanis Club.

I slept for over twelve hours in a very comfortable bed and had a large delicious breakfast on Sunday morning. Every waitress at the Cracker Barrel came over to talk to me and wished me well. The managers both came by and talked with me, and several of the customers talked with me also.

I left Seymour with a great feeling of friendship. I was feeling tired and unwanted when I left Versailles, but I left Seymour feeling that I was doing something important by walking across this country.

*****

Before I left on my walk the Kiwanis International did a write-up about my walk and it was sent to all the officers of all the Clubs. I assumed most of the officers would be aware of my walk. I was wrong.

One interesting experience was in Indiana. On a Sunday afternoon I was about eight miles from Bedford when I called Bill, the president of the Bedford Kiwanis Club. A young girl answered and I told her who I was and she said her father was playing golf and would return shortly. I told her I would call when I arrived in town. Shortly after seven I arrived in town and called, but I was only able to talk to a recording machine. I assumed that Bill would be home shortly, so I left the message that I would wait for him at Burger King, which was just down the street.

I asked the manager of the Burger King if there was another Burger King in town and he told me there was not. I waited, had a couple salads and finally became concerned as to where I was going to spend the night if Bill didn't come.

Around 9:30 I noticed two couples at the next table. I struck up a conversation and asked if they were local. They said they were so I asked them if they knew any Kiwanians in town. One of the men said he knew Bill.

I explained my circumstances and he nodded knowingly. He introduced himself as John. He tried to call Bill, but he got the same answering machine I had talked with earlier. This lack of response did not bother him. He turned to me, waved toward the parking lot and said, "Get your pack and come with me." I felt much better knowing I now had a place to stay. I wasn't sure where it was, but I felt much better. He drove me to Bedford Community Hospital, took me into Receiving, told the nurse on duty, "Check him in and charge it to Bill." She did.

A nurse took me to a room in the very rear of the hospital, a room with a shower and an excellent bed. I showered and about eleven I went out to the nurse's station and asked to talk to the Head Nurse. The Head Nurse was an attractive brunette with close cut hair. She wore large metal-rimmed glasses with a double metal bridge across her nose. We went back to my room and I asked her, "Do you know why I'm here?"

She answered, "I was wondering what you are doing here?"

"Well," I said. "I'm a member of the Kiwanis Club. I was trying to reach Bill and John gave me ..."

The nurse raised her hand to stop me. She smiled the smile of a cat with a captured prey. "Everyone has to hear this."

She returned with several other nurses and then asked me to tell them how I got there. I did. The nurses enjoyed the story very much because Bill was the chief financial officer of the hospital. They mentioned how they were constantly questioned about expenditures, and yet I was staying the night compliments of Bill. They all thanked me, wished me well and went about their duties.

The next morning I rose, showered and went to the cafeteria for a delicious breakfast. I waited in my room and about 8:30 Bill arrived. I am certain that Bill was unhappy, but he hid it well. With his arm extended he motioned toward the door. I picked up my pack, strapped it on and walked out. He walked close to my left side with his right arm behind me, pushing me lightly ahead. As we hurried down the hall we talked briefly about Kiwanis and the activities of their Kiwanis Club. They were very active in several areas and involved in helping victims of a recent tornado.

At the front door of the hospital he waited until I started to walk away. He turned to enter the door again when I asked, "John, the Kiwanian who brought me to the hospital last night, where is he?"

Bill did not smile. He said, "John is no Kiwanian. He's a damned Rotarian!"

Illinois

Illinois

The Wabash River separated Indiana from Illinois and I was now on the bridge over the Wabash. The Wabash was not as wide as the Delaware nor did it move as fast. It did appear to have more dirt. As I crossed the bridge into Illinois I saw a large statue of Abraham Lincoln. This was my introduction to the 'Land of Lincoln.'

As I entered Illinois I met another man walking the roads of the United States. A thin, heavy-bearded man about forty carrying a twenty-five foot wooden cross over his shoulder. The end of the cross was on wheels, but he carried a heavy load. He said he was walking back and forth across the United States carrying "the message." He asked if I had been saved. I lied and said I was. I was afraid if I said I wasn't he would follow me all the way to California.

West of Sandoval I met a man about my age riding a bicycle. He lived in Shattuck, only five miles away. He said that he bicycled forty miles per day for exercise. He looked very trim and well-tanned. He invited me to spend the night at his house, but I declined; it was too early in the day to stop. He was pedaling in shorts with no shirt and his tan glowed a warm red. I had worn a shirt my entire trip and used sunblock on most days when the sky was clear. The sun was great for plants, but I didn't want to get skin cancer from my walk. The bicyclist merely said that since he was going to die anyway, why worry. I prefer to try to protect myself as much as practical in the hope of living longer.

Between Lebanon and O'Fallon, Illinois, I met several people. I was offered more rides in those ten miles than I had received on any day previously. At one point, there were three cars stopped and all three drivers were offering me rides. I declined the first two; one was a large family crowded into a small car and the other offer was from a man with a bottle of beer in his hand. The third was a serviceman, Gerald, who wanted some company as he headed home to St. Louis. As we drove toward O'Fallon I understood why knowledgeable drivers were offering me rides. For over four miles the road was narrow with no shoulder. There was six foot drop-off to water on either side of the road. There was an odor that indicated it had been there for several weeks. I was glad I was riding across such a bad stretch of road. When we had crossed the narrow portion, he dropped me off but he insisted that I take two cans of Pepsi and a sandwich with me.

As I went to bed that evening near the Mississippi River I reflected on my walk. In crossing the United States I had set certain goals, certain achievements that I considered important. My first goal on this trip had been the crossing of the Appalachian Mountains. The next goal had been crossing the Ohio River. Tomorrow I would cross the Mississippi River. I was approaching half way across the United States. Well, I was over one-third of the way. Half way would be somewhere in Kansas, still a couple weeks away. After Kansas the next goal would be crossing the Rocky Mountains and that was a long, long way west. Beyond that was the Sierra Nevada Mountains and finally San Francisco and the Golden Gate Bridge. That bridge seemed a long way away tonight.

Missouri

Missouri

Sunday afternoon was exceptionally warm and the air was very moist. I made it to Gray Summit, Missouri, and found a room in the Daniel Boone Motel for the night. It was a rainy, stormy night with lightning, thunder, and, I was told, a tornado watch. I was too tired to watch and went to bed.

This was Father's Day and also the day my daughter, Doreen, was to receive her Master's Degree from UCLA. Doreen was in my thoughts a lot that day because her world was in front of her and she had the ability to obtain a position of importance. I also thought about Yvonne because she allowed her errant husband to wander around the country, and I thought about my other two daughters, Karen and Shirley. I was a lucky person to have such a wonderful family.

It was five weeks ago that I started this trip. In five weeks I had met several great people and seen a lot of this great country. But the most important thing I had learned was my own capabilities. I could endure! When the walk began, I hurt everywhere, felt miserable and often my feet were swollen and painful, but I had endured and the pain subsided and the world improved. I knew I could walk across this country. I could do anything I wanted to do, because I could persevere.

I slept very little Sunday night at Gray Summit because the rain was very heavy at times and the thunder was often loud. The power in the motel was interrupted so my room became very hot and muggy. Then the emergency vehicles started running up and down the road with their sirens and horns blasting the sleep from anyone close by. I never did find out what happened, but since it didn't happen to me or anyone I knew, I was probably better off keeping out off the way. I did have the thought that the firemen brought all their kids to the fire station for Father's Day, loaded them on fire trucks and drove them around town with the tremendous noise-makers shrieking just to celebrate the holiday.

Monday afternoon I reached Union, Missouri, and decided that was far enough. My pack was beginning to tear in several places so I got that fixed at Carson's Shoe Repair. My other problem was water containers, or lack of. I had brought only one water container, a one quart flask. Richard Sandoval, the president of the Union Kiwanis Club, gave me two additional one quart flasks that served me well. As I started my walk on Tuesday I noticed the increased weight. Two additional containers amounted to four more pounds. I welcomed the refreshment, but they sure were heavy.

*****

I made it on Tuesday to Owensville. On the way to Owensville, about two miles east of Rosebud, a pickup stopped. The driver, a thin, stringy-haired blond about thirty, asked me if I wanted a ride. I told her no, that I was walking. She told me to get in the back. I again said no, that I was walking.

She yelled to me, "Get your ass in the back of the truck." I didn't feel I had a choice. If I did not get in I was certain she was going to get out of that truck and put me in it. I got in. In the back of the truck was a large tire which I used as a comfortable recliner.

She drove about two miles down the road to Rosebud, stopped and yelled back at me, "That's the end of it. Get out." I did. I thanked her and started to ask her for her name and she turned to me and said, "If you'd walk on our side of the road, you'd get more rides. Hear me?" She then drove down a side street and stopped.

I stayed on 'our' side of the road until I was out of sight of her truck, then I changed back to the left side, facing traffic. About fifteen minutes later the same pickup stopped again, same woman. I knew I was going to be reprimanded for being on the wrong side.

She yelled across the road, "You really are walking ain't you? Come over here and get in." I did. I had already learned not to argue with this woman. The first time she had picked me up there was a young girl riding with her; this time she was alone.

She introduced herself as Ellie and said she raised hogs, "not the kind you eat every day, but a special kind."

"Pet hogs?" I asked, knowing this was a micro-fad among the too rich.

"No." she told me. "They're for eating, but there's not much meat on them. But they sure pay well. There's only two hundred twenty hogs like this in the country."

As we sat in her car I asked her if she was married. She said, "Yep! Three times. The first one I divorced. The second one died." She looked at me with suspicion. "So I'm on my third one." Ellie was a very sharp woman. Her vocabulary was back country, but her mind was precise.

We talked for about ten or fifteen minutes I asked her to write her name in my book. "And," I added. "Would you give me the name of your daughter who was riding with you."

Ellie asked why and I explained that I was going to write a book about my trip and I was going to include the names of the people I had met. She wrote the two names, nodded and left.

A short time later she came back. She said, "This is my other daughter. It's important that her name be in your book. She wants to be a writer." I took her name and then Ellie and I talked for a while. She explained that her second husband hadn't really died, she had killed him, "Because he had tried to kill me." She told me she was going to write a book about that.

I must have displayed some apprehension about her book. She added, "He was already a murderer." Now, I decided, she had a good book. She was straightforward and honest. If I were in an argument or a fight and I was right, I would like to have her on my side.

In Owensville I found a cheap motel, took a shower and lay down to rest. I rested for a while but my stomach was complaining. I realized I had eaten very little that day. I got up, dressed and went out to find a restaurant. I found a great deal. All you can eat for $3.99. I entered and paid my $3.99 plus tax. The meal was spaghetti, roll and a salad. I found out early in my trip that it did not pay to eat fast, so I did not eat fast. I went through the line six times. Each time I took very little, probably about a third of a meal, so my six times was the equivalent of two meals.

As I was finishing up my sixth small meal the manager came over, introduced himself and sat down. "Where are you from?" He asked.

"Sonora, California," I said. "I'm walking across the United States." I showed him a clipping from The Union Democrat. He ignored the clipping.

"You don't live around here, then?" he asked

"No," I replied.

I continued eating. I went through the line three more times. It was now three hours of eating, and I was full. I had talked to a lot of people, drank a lot of water and gone to the rest room three times.

As I started to leave, the manager came up to me. "You live in California?

"Yes"

"You don't live around here."

"That's right."

"When you get home," the manager said. "See your doctor. You have a tapeworm."

*****

On the first day of summer I walked down Missouri Route 28 to Belle. It was only fifteen miles for the day. The countryside was still hilly with lots of pastures and few cattle. The red barns and white houses of Pennsylvania were past. Instead there were old houses and older barns, many unpainted.

There were several ponds along the road, many with fish. Some were fenced for livestock, others were just for fishing with chairs or stools. There was a great deal of grass around all the houses, most well mowed and well maintained. Riding mowers were probably a necessity because of the size of the fields.

As I approached Belle, a lady stepped from her house and invited me in for a cold drink. I had plenty of time so I accepted the invitation. The lady who invited me in was from Maryland. I decided she was about fifty-eight, since she commented that she was going to her fortieth reunion. Her mother, eighty-eight, was there also. She had come down to Belle to bury her husband. I sat in the cool comfort of their home for about an hour and drank three glasses of ice-cold water. Both of the ladies were very alert and very nice. Two of the many enjoyable people that made my walk so much nicer.

One of the gifts I received before I left Sonora, from the Kiwanis Club of Sonora, was a AAA insurance policy for roadside service. If my car failed on the road, all I had to do was call AAA, and they would pick me up.

This was a valuable service, if you were driving, but I didn't really need it. The other service it provided was maps. These were valuable.

I thought I would find how valuable my AAA was for roadside service. I stopped at a service station in Belle that offered the 'AAA Service.' I asked the owner what would happen if I called in.

"Well," he pondered. "If I came out and you had a car, we'd have no problem. If there weren't no car, you and I'd have a long talk."

He didn't answer my problem, but I never called the AAA either. We talked for a while. I went to the motel next door for a room but they were full. I returned to the service station and asked if they had any suggestions. They did.

They went down the street and talked to the Marshall. He had them send me to the ballpark to sleep. I was assured there was nothing going on that night at the ballpark, and that I would be under cover.

They were right, I was under cover. But they were wrong, there was something going on that night, a little league game. It was played in the rain, complete with parents and screaming kids. The game began at eight o'clock; it didn't end until after eleven, with a final score of 39 to 38, and it rained for three hours.

"We don't call a game unless it's lightning." The official explained when I asked about the rain. It didn't lightning much, but I didn't sleep much either.

The next morning there were a couple old men collecting aluminum cans and talking too loudly so I was awakened at five. I washed up with cold water in the men's room and shaved. There was no toilet paper in the rest room, but I had some in my pack. I walked the two miles to Belle, had breakfast and headed down Missouri Route 28 for Rolla.

*****

The weather Tuesday was the same as it had been most days, very changeable. I heard several times in Missouri that if you don't like the weather now, be patient, in an hour it will change. I believed it. I had rain, bright sun, beautiful clouds, wind, calm, and various mixtures of the above. The farmers I talked with were never happy with the weather. This year was entirely too wet. The wheat had rust and mildew. The rain delayed getting the corn in.

There were times along the road that I felt almost guilty. On the day into Rolla, I was sitting at the side of the road watching the clouds blowing across the sky. Their shapes changed quickly and with imagination I could see lions, horses, buildings and cars. I recalled the song, "Sitting at the dock of the bay, watching the tide rolling in." That was how I felt, just relaxed, calm and enjoying life.

Rolla, from a distance, appeared like the Emerald City in the Wizard of Oz. I stood at the side of the road admiring the view. The discouraging view was just to the left, a materials handling facility with piles of various substances and dust over everything.

After I had dinner and was walking up the stairs to my room, I struck up a conversation with a couple also walking up the stairs. They were drinking coffee and they asked if I would like a cup. I said I would and they invited me into their room.

He introduced himself as Roger. He appeared a little overweight and definitely not in good physical shape. His handshake was weak and when he walked up the stairs I noticed it was with significant effort. The lady poured me a cup of coffee and Roger and I were talking about the heat.

As we continued talking, Roger asked if I drank. I said I did. He asked what I liked to drink. I told him red wine was preferred. He looked rather sullen and asked if I had a second choice. I said I did, scotch. He smiled and asked if I would like a scotch. I agreed, without any additional arm twisting.

Roger went into the bathroom and returned with a glass of scotch over several ice cubes. It tasted great. We talked and finally Roger told me that since I was taking a few days off to go to the convention, I should take some scotch with me. It sounded pretty good to me. Roger invited me into his bathroom.

In his small bathtub he had at least fifty bottles of whiskey of all types and brands. He had the making of a complete bar, except for the wine and beer. I wondered where he took his bath, since the bottles would be difficult to remove every day. I didn't ask him. I also wondered where the whiskey came from, but decided not to ask that question either.

He filled one of my one-quart containers with good blended scotch. Roger never told me how he earned his living and he was one of the few people who didn't give me his name for my book. He was just Roger, and he never gave me the name of the woman with him, and neither did she. I finished my glass of scotch, rejected the offer of another, and went to bed and slept very well.

I rode the bus back to St. Louis on Saturday afternoon. Time for me to attend the Kiwanis International Convention in St. Louis.

Kiwanis Convention

Kiwanis Convention

Kiwanis is a Service Club much like the Lions Clubs or the Rotary Clubs. Being a member of a service Club was often inconvenient and at times very difficult. But it was also very rewarding. I visited about thirty Kiwanis Clubs from New York City to Palo Alto, California. Members of the Kiwanis Clubs arranged motels for me or invited me to their homes. They fed me, and fed me well. They arranged for me to get repairs and pick up supplies. They made the walk much easier.

I was promoting a Kiwanis Program, 'KNOW TO SAY NO,' a drug education program aimed at grade school children. Every Kiwanis Club I visited I talked for about fifteen minutes about the program. I believed in it.

I found it interesting that the Kiwanis Clubs I visited were all significantly different. Some met in fancy restaurants, some met in a member's home, others met in churches and one met in a bar. But they all worked hard for their communities. They were all striving to make the world a little better off for their having been here. They were good people.

Now I was going to the Kiwanis International Convention. I had never been to a convention of any type before, so I was looking forward to St. Louis and the Kiwanis International Convention. I had talked to Bill Lacey, the Lieutenant Governor from the Sonora area, and planned to meet him at the Clarion Hotel. I arrived before he did, so I went down to the Convention Center to pick up my packet, a bunch of paper and my admission information.

Upon entering the Convention Center two hearty souls from the Operation KNOW program, Philip and Jim, saw me and dragged me to their booth. They displayed absolute enthusiasm for my walking across the United States for their program. I spent the next three days with Philip and Jim as well as a few others, Steve, Jack, Brent and Darlene. They were enthusiastic about Operation KNOW and they worked very hard for it.

The majority of my time at the convention was spent at the Operation KNOW booth telling people about the program and encouraging them to look at it closely. The best salesperson for the program was not me, or Philip, or Jim or even Steve. It was Drug Free.

Drug Free was a robot. At least I think he was a robot. He got more hugs from the women than I did, and all the kids that came by really liked him. He had an exceptional personality, thanks to Jack. I liked Drug Free and his use in the program was significant to the reception of the program. When he comes to the Sonora Kiwanis Club, I want to make him a member of our Club, if Jack will just pay his dues.

I was impressed by the enthusiasm of the crew of Operation KNOW, but the delegates at the convention impressed me in a different way. There were grown men and women, mostly men, wearing outlandish hats, vests and jackets of several different colors, displaying their Kiwanis colors. Many of the delegates had matching costumes. The delegation from CalNevHa, composed of California, Nevada and Hawaii, were encouraged to wear a particular pattern of an aloha shirt. Some of the other delegations had matching green vests, others had yellow hats. It gave the appearance of a huge carnival.

Some of the delegates also had pins. They had pins on their hats, vests and jackets. Some delegates were trading pins constantly. On the second day I was talking to Arnold, a Canadian who displayed enthusiasm for my walk. He gave me a pin, with the Canadian flag, to wear. I wore it proudly because I have always felt that Canada was the best friend the United States has in this world, and they have often displayed their friendship without reservations.

A few hours after I fastened the Canadian pin on my shirt, a Kiwanian with lots of pins on his vest saw it and his offering began. At first he would only offer me two of his pins for my Canadian pin. He wanted my Canadian pin, because he ended with an offer that I could have any eight pins from his collection of over a hundred, in exchange for my Canadian pin.

He had hundreds of beautiful pins. Large ones with emblems of states on them. He had multicolored pins in several different shapes. He did have a couple pins I would have enjoyed. One showed Donald Duck flying a jet. It had great colors and design. Another I liked had all the flags of the Americas on it. It was well done also. His pins had no real significant value to me, and the Canadian pin did, so no transaction took place. I kept my pin. I have two other pins, a Kansas sunflower and a patriotism pin. The Kansas pin I received from a friend I met from Kansas and the patriotism pin I earned before leaving California.

Ribbons as well as pins were also displayed at the convention, wide colorful ribbons that hung from the badges. There were several different colors of ribbons and each ribbon denoted something of importance in the Kiwanis organization: delegate, Lieutenant Governor, District Governor and positions such as that. There were also ribbons for having donated certain sums to the Kiwanis Foundation.

The convention was a place for the delegates to get together with other delegates and lie about their Club's achievements, their families and their cities. I recalled life in Navy boot camp many, many years before when you had to invent new lies just to keep up with the previous lies. I learned not to believe anything I heard at the convention.

A Kiwanian from Alabama said, "Our popcorn fund-raiser netted us over three thousand dollars!" Think how many boxes of popcorn sold to net three thousand dollars!

The tall gawky Kiwanian from Texas claimed, "Our Kiwanis Club has all the important people in town!" I have a problem with 'all' the important people. It may have been a club of one and he considered himself the most important person in town.

The meek, young, little lady from Washington exclaimed, "We never have any problems finding new officers, we are all leaders!" Yeah, sure????

The short, overweight man from Florida said, "We don't have a problem with people quitting. Our problem is deciding which applicants we want in our club!" I felt he may have had a problem, but didn't know it.

I enjoyed the bragging, and I felt that I could keep up with the best. It was easy since I was from Sonora, which was the best place in the world to live, and we had the finest Club in all Kiwanis.

*****

It was during the convention that I changed my planned route through Kansas. Larry Tucker, who had been the Kiwanis District Governor of Kansas, showed me the best route to take. He showed me the roads with the widest shoulders, the least traffic and the most Kiwanis Clubs. His directions helped a lot.

Because of the efforts of Steve and Philip, I was introduced to a meeting of the delegates by the International President of Kiwanis, Noris A. Lusche. They had intended for me to be introduced from the floor, but I walked up the stairs, walked to the front of the stage and shook hands with Noris A. Lusche. I felt I deserved that much recognition. I received a standing ovation when I gave the delegates a thumbs up, turned and showed them my pack. I appreciated that ovation. President Lusche was very smart in not allowing me to talk to the delegates. I had a short speech about drugs, Kiwanis and our way of life. Since I didn't get to talk to them it didn't matter.

I also went to a baseball game between the Cardinals and the Mets. A few years back, in Visalia, California, I lived next door to Bobby

Ojeda, who was now a pitcher for the Mets. After the game I found him at a nearby bar and we talked briefly. He hasn't changed from when I met him. He still acted like a ballplayer.

The Operation KNOW program was initiated in Georgia and resided in Georgia. Thanks to the efforts of Philip and Jack, I went to the dinner for the Georgia delegation. It was held aboard a paddle wheel steamboat. Due to the flood conditions on the Mississippi it never left the dock, but I met several fine Kiwanians from Georgia and everyone had a delicious steak dinner.

I also saw St. Louis' downtown shopping center in the old Union Station. The shopping center was a fantastic idea and because of the way the shops were grouped it was easy to find what I wanted to see. It was also designed for easy visibility so I felt very comfortable walking around the station. They did a good job. The Arch gave me a thrill and was a major architectural accomplishment.

I was most impressed in St. Louis by the manner in which I was treated. The Arch and Union Station were great for drawing people to St. Louis, but the people I met made me want to return.

The Kiwanians joked around a lot and often appeared to be very shallow and selfish. I'm sure some were, but the majority were not. The whole purpose of the Kiwanis organization was to help others. At the convention the members collected pins and wore ribbons to show their distinction, but when they go home they invest their effort to make their cities better places to live and work and make their neighborhoods better places to raise children. I harassed a lot of the Kiwanians at the convention, but I was very proud to be a Kiwanian.

On the next to last day of the convention I sent word to the Kansas delegation that I needed a ride to Nevada, Missouri. I had to make up for the time I had spent at the Kiwanis convention. Thanks to the District Governors of California and Kansas, I had the help I needed. John and Lucy who lived in western Kansas offered to take me to Nevada, Missouri, the next morning. I had rested long enough. I was anxious to get back on the road again.

The last night in St. Louis, I shared the last of my scotch, ate a huge meal and discussed the convention with Jim. I had met many great people and had renewed my belief in Kiwanis and in Operation KNOW. I was glad I came to the convention, but it was time to leave. The rest in St. Louis caused my feet and ankles to swell and they hurt more just standing around than they did when I walked. I wanted to leave, and tomorrow I would. I missed the walking, but I missed home more.

I missed Yvonne of course, but I also missed the bookstore, particularly the odor of the bookstore. As I crossed the country I often went into used bookstores and found that there was an odor that was only in used bookstores. I missed that odor. It would also be nice to not have to live out of my pack. I knew where everything was in my pack, but it sure would be nice to walk into the kitchen and get a Pepsi from the fridge instead of out of the bottom of my pack. The idea that I didn't know where I would be spending the next night was also a problem. It would be nice to go to sleep in our bed and know that I will be able to do that for the next several nights. I guess it was love that I missed. Yvonne and I had been together for nearly thirty-three years. In that time we have had some problems, but we worked them out. Most of our time had been great, truly great. It was this love that I missed and I knew this love was at home. I also knew the only way I would get home was to resume my walking.

(Photos by Santa Clara Valley Weekly)

Clouds Over Craig, Colorado

Creators of Roadside Turbulence

A Big Goal I Met

Hotel With an Unusual Owner

Trail Ridge, Colorado Rockies

Almost Home
(Photo by Sonora Union Democrat)

The Finish with Yvonne and Matt

Matt and grandson Kevin (Photo by Sonora Union Democrat)

Matt's Sixth Pair of Shoes
(Photo by Sonora
Union Democrat)

Back at Work
(Photo by Sonora
Union Democrat

Western Missouri

Western Missouri

The ride across Missouri from St. Louis to western Missouri with John and Lucy was an experience I will always remember. In Missouri the first 'A' in Nevada is pronounced with a hard 'A' as in 'made', not the same as the state Nevada with a soft 'A.'

I have learned in life to cover my real feelings with various masks. I wear one mask in front of my children, another for the neighbors, another for the customers, etc. John and Lucy were two of the most sincere people I have ever met. They were incapable of wearing a mask. They were the same to me as they would have been to George Bush, to their daughter or to the guy next door. They were down home simple folks from Kansas.

They had asked me to meet them at nine in the morning. I was there three minutes early and we left immediately. I had not had breakfast but the ride was important to me so I said nothing as we set out from St. Louis. Lucy began talking and she never quit. John always had a slight grin on his face, as if he knew what Lucy was going to say next. He probably did after being married to her for forty years.

"See that orange flower?" Lucy asked as we drove down Interstate 70 at fifty miles per hour. "I call that flower a snake flower. I know that's not its real name, but one time, when us girls were bringing in the cows, I saw a rattlesnake in amongst those orange flowers. That's why I call it a snake flower."

During the five hour trip she told me about "this, that and t'other," and I hung on every word. John was the Kiwanis Lieutenant Governor for the area of Kansas where I was going He said he would contact the people in Ft. Scott for me. John and Lucy were real great Kansas people.

They dropped me off at the Post Office in Nevada, Missouri. Lucy wanted John to wait and take me to a motel. I assured her I could find a place to sleep. John wanted to get home, because he had been gone a long time and he had things to do. The ride had helped me a great deal and I was once more ready to get on the road. I was looking forward to the exercise of walking, of walking fast with a pack on my back. I enjoyed walking and I had missed it.

I picked up my mail and returned a package back to Sonora. I received a pair of Levis, my wife's Levis. The Levis I had started with had become too large and slipped down too easily. I had lost ten pounds getting ready for the walk. Since I had begun my walk two months ago I had lost another twenty pounds. The walk was great as a weight-loss program. Yvonne sent me her pair until she could buy a new pair, wash them and send them to me. I also mailed home some extra T-shirts and anything else I could find to lower the weight of my pack.

I picked up several letters. My wife told me all was well. I appreciated hearing that. Karen's letter told me she was getting bigger. She included a letter from Kevin, her son, and my greatest grandson. Kevin wanted to know about the snake in Pennsylvania. He wanted to know if I met any other mean dogs. He said he missed me. I missed him too.

Doreen's letter said she had graduated from UCLA with her Master's Degree and understood my not being there. She made it clear that if I wanted to come home, that I should. She said that I didn't have to walk all the way, if I didn't want to. She said she loved me and missed me.

I received a letter from Leetta, one of the members of the Kiwanis Club of Sonora. She told me all about the Club and she included some money for me to, "spend in such a manner that it would help me enjoy my walk."

Kansas

Kansas

I stayed that night in a motel in Nevada, Missouri, and left for Kansas early the next morning. I had not suffered any really intense heat in the first 1500 miles of my walk. In Missouri it had been warm, but never really hot. When I crossed the Kansas state line, the temperature went up ten degrees. It was hot in Kansas, too hot for an old man walking.

Before I left Sonora I had a complete checkup including a treadmill test. My doctor told me to keep my pulse below one hundred forty on the walk and I would have no trouble. He said I could handle one hundred fifty for a short time. Most of the time as I walked my pulse was around ninety. The heat of Kansas raised my pulse to about one hundred twenty as I walked three and a half miles per hour. My shoulders, where the pack rested, became wet with collected moisture. My waistband was also wet. I slowed my pace and that helped a little.

I arrived at the outskirts of Ft. Scott at a small drive-in, Bright's Grill, and called the Kiwanis President, Mark. He had never heard of me so I explained who I was and why I was there. He told me that he was usually on the road and that I was very lucky to contact him. Mark invited me to spend the night at his house and said he would be down in about a half hour. That was fine. The owners of Bright's Grill treated me to a meal and called the local press. When Mark came, the press had not yet arrived so Mark made a call, and a reporter soon arrived.

In my walk I found there were numbers to call for the press. Those were important contacts, and if you didn't know those contacts no one ever came. These contacts were not in the phone directory, nor could you find them by asking. You had to know someone at the paper. The owner was best but the editor was all right, too. A reporter or photographer were next, and usually sufficient. A clerk, secretary or a gofer were not worthwhile. Mark knew a reporter. The owners of the drive-in only knew the phone number.

The initial reason that I had decided to go through Ft. Scott was to see the town where my mother was born, Savonburg, Kansas. I was orphaned at the age of fourteen and I had never met anyone from my mother's side of the family. Maybe one of her relatives would still be there. I checked the phone book and there was no one listed with the last name of Richardson, my mother's maiden name. Mark drove me to Savonburg that evening.

I'm not sure what I expected in Savonburg, but I was disappointed. Savonburg was just an old railroad town, dying at the side of a gravel road. Mark let me look around and he took my picture in front of the Post Office. An interesting thought crossed my mind that many of the old trees I was looking at had been viewed by my mother when she was a child. It was not what I had expected, but I had seen it and tomorrow I would continue on my long walk home.

*****

Early Saturday morning Mark dropped me off on the road to Iola and wished me well. It was a good day, but it was hot. I intended to walk thirty-three miles that day, but the heat got to me. About seven miles from Iola a car, headed toward Iola, stopped and the driver got out.

I didn't wait for his question, I just said, "Yes." The driver was a reporter from the Iola Register and he had come out to interview me. "Not here," I told him. "It's too hot!"

We held the interview in his air-conditioned office in Iola. The reporter did impress me because he was the only reporter who called my wife to get her reaction to my walk. He wrote a good article. From the Iola Register office, I called the local Kiwanis member, Bob. He came down and picked me up and the reporter followed us out to Bob's house to get a picture. I spent the evening at Bob's home and his wife repaired my pack where it was tearing again.

It was forty miles to Eureka from Iola and Bob was concerned about my walking that far in the heat. It was hot, even by Kansas terms. Early the next morning Bob took me a ways out, about ten miles, and sent me on my way to Eureka on another very hot day, a hot day without any breeze.

About mid-morning I met another hardy trooper traveling the byways of our country, Kathy. A young woman bicycling from Connecticut to Seattle, Washington. Kathy was a very attractive girl about twenty-three, an exuberant and bubbly person who enjoyed life and all it offered her. She was proud of what she was doing and my faith in the people of the United States increased considerably knowing that a young woman could still travel across our country without being accosted. Our television and newspapers lead us to believe something quite different.

This was the hottest day I had seen so far. About four miles from Eureka I stopped and was about to take a long rest when a truck stopped and the driver asked if I wanted a ride into town. I accepted the ride and felt no pangs of guilt. It was too hot to walk.

In Eureka I called Dan, the Kiwanis' President. Dan came in from his farm, about seven miles from town, and picked me up. Dan was a big man and a very outgoing individual. Dan's size, personality and general demeanor were similar to that of John Wayne. During the evening I often thought of the similarity.

Dan took me to the race track first. In Eureka they have a race track, with parimutuel betting, and apparently Dan was a part of the money, or perhaps the inspiration, behind the track. He introduced me to several people he knew, and he invited all of them to his house for hamburgers and watermelon later that day. Most accepted.

That evening I was interviewed by a very intelligent and competent young woman, who worked for the local radio station. Several people came over for the hamburgers and watermelon. Dan's father-in-law came out. He remarked that he had passed me during the day and he had suggested to his wife that anyone walking from New York to San Francisco on such a hot day must have a vacancy between his ears. He was probably correct.

Dan raised some cattle on the farm where he lived, he was in real estate and he was an auctioneer and did many of the local auctions. His wife was also a real estate agent and a first grade teacher. Dan explained that it took more than one income, and usually more than one job, to live these days. It was true in Kansas and it was true everywhere else in our country.

Dan's home was the house where he was born and raised. He had enlarged and improved it considerably, and it was very comfortable. Dan was very gracious and enjoyable. During the evening Dan made a statement that I had heard before. We were sitting outside by the huge lawn, the sun was about to go down and there was a soft breeze. Dan suggested that this was the most wonderful place in the world. And he believed it. So did I.

I had heard that same statement in New Jersey at Pete Johnson's house and again in Ft. Loudon, Pennsylvania, from Kris and Will. Karl had said it in New Hope, Pennsylvania, and I would hear it a few more times on this long walk home.

I slept well that evening and early Monday morning Dan took me to town, bought me a delicious breakfast of biscuits, gravy and a side of sausage, at The City Cafe. With my stomach full, Dan sent me on my way to El Dorado. Dan assured me he would call the Kiwanis in El Dorado.

I read Voltaire's Candide and was familiar with the land of El Dorado, but in Kansas, El Dorado is pronounced with a hard 'A' as in 'made.' There was nothing between Eureka and El Dorado but heat. I had expected flat farm land, but I was mistaken. It was more like Texas than the Kansas I had recalled. When I mentioned this to a local rancher he said that he had heard that Texas was a lot like Kansas. There were only a few cultivated fields and a lot of pasture land.

About the time I was in this cattle country, K.T. Oslin, an excellent female western singer, recorded a song about 'Don't eat beef' and it bothered a lot of the cattle people. I was told the local radio station would not play anything by her on their station.

The hills here were referred to as the 'foothills.' I asked what they were the foot to, but I never got an answer. I hoped there weren't some mountains ahead that I didn't know about. I was still looking for that flat land I had been told was just ahead. In a car maybe it was flat, but walking it was not flat. It wasn't even close.

I arrived at a cafe on the outskirts of El Dorado about five-thirty. I called the local Kiwanis president, but there was no answer. I called the secretary and he suggested I call the Lieutenant Governor. I did and I heard a recorded message that he had already sold the car, but he still had two boats for sale. I struck up a conversation with a couple of the locals. I asked them if they knew a Kiwanian in El Dorado. One of the locals mentioned that he had just seen Sharon going into a restaurant. They assured me Sharon was a Kiwanian and they took me down to the restaurant and introduced us.

Sharon and her husband were just finishing dinner as we came in. Almost immediately, they invited me to spend the night at their home. I accepted, thanked the two locals and went with Sharon and her husband to their home in downtown El Dorado. It was one of the most spacious, inviting, almost opulent, homes I had seen. It was on the second floor above some small businesses. They had converted four apartments into a beautiful home.

Finally that evening, I got hold of the president, Dick. Since the Kiwanis meeting was on Tuesday evening, the next day, he said he would pick me up twenty miles west of El Dorado at Buffalo Corners and he would bring me back to the meeting. Sharon invited me to spend the next night at her house also so it sounded great to me.

Early in the evening we drove around El Dorado, past the oil refinery and around El Dorado Lake. Sharon and I stayed up until past twelve Monday night talking.

*****

Early Tuesday morning I set out for Buffalo Corners. Shortly after noon I decided to take a break, but the only shade was about forty feet up a side road. As I crossed and started up the road a car came toward me. It was a sheriff's car with red and blue lights flashing. I stepped aside to let it past, but it stopped. The deputy stepped out. He was broad shouldered, had a large seven-pointed star on his chest, with neatly pressed shirt and trousers. I knew his car was air conditioned. He asked me who I was and what was I doing there. I explained, but he didn't believe me. He asked for some identification. Sarcastically I said I had a 'walker's license,' but he didn't think that was funny. I gave him my California driver's license and he returned to his car. Another more pleasant deputy stayed and we walked to the shade tree and I sat down. It took almost twenty minutes for the first deputy to return. He handed me my license and thanked me.

I asked him why he had stopped me. He explained that an elderly man had escaped from a nearby retirement home during the night. With my pack on my back I guess I looked like I was running away from home. I asked the deputy if the guy who escaped was a little crazy. He said he was, so I admitted he had probable cause to stop me. I was a little crazy too. That was the first time that I had been questioned and checked out by law enforcement people. At least I knew I didn't have a warrant out for my arrest. Later, in Utah, I would have another confrontation with a highway patrol officer.

After they left I rested for a while. As I sat there, in the shade, I saw a wild turkey in the bushes, a first for me. I was expecting something like a sage hen in size, but this was a big bird, as big as the turkeys grown to eat on Thanksgiving. I also found out that flies in Kansas bite, and they were quick to do it, too.

The type of tree I was resting under, I was told the previous day by a twelve year old, was an Osage Orange, or Hedge tree. It grew large balls called hedge apples, which were apparently useless for anything but reproduction and throwing at teachers.

When I arrived at Buffalo Corners the only store in town was closed. There had been a hurricane wind that blew through here about ten days before I arrived. The owner of the store was working on a messed up pile of lumber. The pile of lumber had been part of his house. He didn't know where the other part was. I asked if it was a tornado. He said it wasn't a tornado, just a wind. He said in a tornado the wind blows in circles. The wind that blew in Buffalo corners was over a hundred twenty miles an hour, but it was only blowing in one direction.

The owner let me in his store where it was reasonably cool and I had a Pepsi, but he had no Twinkies. Later, his wife, Dorothy, came by. She told me that when the wind blew ten days ago she was sure she was going to be blown to Oz. I will always remember her, Dorothy from Kansas.

As arranged, Dick picked me up and drove me back to El Dorado for the Kiwanis meeting. Dick was a tall gawky man. His bib overalls and his thin frame made him appear to be taller. He seldom smiled and when he did it was short and slight.

I spent the night with Sharon and her husband again and early Wednesday morning, July 4th, Dick and his wife, Nancy, picked me up and drove me past Buffalo Corners to Newton. Nancy wanted to be a librarian and she would have been ideal. Her language was exact and proper. On the way we drove through the town of Potwin. I asked what it was named after. Nancy turned to me and said, "You have just sparked my inquisitive mind." She wrote something in her note book. When I go through El Dorado again I will stop and ask Nancy about Potwin and I am certain she will know what it is named for and when it was named.

From Newton I headed west on US 50 to Hutchinson. It was hot, very hot, and I was not moving very fast. Normally I walked at about three and a half miles per hour average. This was the Fourth of July and the temperature in Kansas was about 105 degrees and I was walking about two miles per hour. Luckily, Gene, a member of the Hutchinson Kiwanis, picked me up about 2:30. Sharon had called him to let him know I was coming. I had covered about half of what I wanted, but it was too hot to be concerned. Gene took me to his air conditioned home and introduced me to his wife.

I relaxed for about an hour and then they drove me around Hutchinson and took me to dinner at the Prairie Dunes Country Club. I ate a very large meal. But, with the effort I was spending, I needed the energy. My weight was now at 150, 30 pounds below what it was when I had decided to make this walk and 20 pounds less than when I started the walk.

Gene appeared to be a very conservative person. He walked erect and had a strong handshake. He always looked directly into my eyes when he talked. I liked Gene.

I mentioned pin-trading at the Kiwanis convention. One 'pin' that had been given to me was a Kansas sunflower. It wasn't really a pin, but a sticker. I had it on my pack and I had lost it. Gene called an elderly lady who had attended over fifty Kiwanis International Conventions.

She came over and I got a replacement 'pin.' I listening intently to her reminiscences of early times. She was a beautiful person.

During the evening as we talked, we could hear the fireworks from the Fourth of July celebration, but I was tired so I didn't even go outside to watch them. About ten in the evening the Hutchinson News called and I had an interview over the phone. Early the next morning his wife cooked me a large breakfast of bacon and eggs. After breakfast Gene took me to the radio station for an interview. Larry Tucker, whom I met at the convention, met us at the radio station also. It was nice to talk with him again.

The interview at the radio station, KWBW, went very well. The interviewer commented on how calm I was. I thanked him. My attitude on radio, and later television, interviews was that no one was going to hear it or see it anyway, so there was no reason to worry.

As I walked along the roads, I held several interviews in my mind. I always had the right answers for difficult questions. I answered questions on every subject and constantly showed my vast understanding of the world and my quick wit and uncanny intelligence. I noticed that in a real interview, I lacked much of the wit and all the uncanny intelligence, but I enjoyed interviews anyway.

After the interview, Gene drove me a ways out on Kansas Route 96 and sent me on my way toward Lyons. Gene said he would call the Kiwanis in Lyons for me.

The weather report said it was going to be another hot day, but I did not really believe it. There were a few clouds in the western sky and a slight breeze. Route 96 was a two-lane, no-shoulder road with very little traffic.

Twice during the day I had my adrenaline stirring through my system when a car came very close. I always walk facing traffic so the close car was not a car coming toward me, but a car coming from behind me. It was a car passing another. I was not sure how close the cars came. It could have been six inches or it could have been three feet. I know I was not expecting it and that's why I got so excited. A driver passing another on a two lane road was not watching for an old man walking at the side. He was only looking for the other cars. Most of the time I walked on the shoulder, but an unexpected car going sixty or seventy miles an hour only a foot away raised the level of my attention. That was why I knew bicycle riding was dangerous, all the cars were coming up from behind you.

It turned out to be another very hot day, not as hot as the Fourth, but still hot, even by Kansas standards. A little after two, as I was approaching an entrance to a field, a pickup pulled into the entrance and then backed up the road toward me. The pickup stopped and the driver got out and said, "I'm Jerry from the Lyons Kiwanis Club. I know you're Matt. Get in."

I did, and without any additional coaxing. Jerry and his wife, Bonnie, were babysitting their granddaughter and enjoying it tremendously. Jerry was a high school PE teacher and it was obvious he liked his position. Bonnie asked if I would like to go skiing. I said I would. I knew it would be skiing the natural way—behind a boat. We picked up two teenage girls Jerry was recruiting for his tennis team, and the five of us went water skiing at Kanopolis Lake.

I made a poor showing for a California boy, but I did manage to get up on doubles for a short time. One of the teenagers had skied before and she felt comfortable behind the boat. I helped the other and she did get up for a short ride. Bonnie loved to ski on a single and would have followed the boat all day if Jerry hadn't cut the engine. It was enjoyable and a nice break from walking. Jerry introduced me to some friends and I had an interview with the Lyons Daily News.

Jerry's interaction with the teenagers was professional, caring and very effective. He was their teacher, not a friend, but at the same time he listened to their troubles and gave them advice. He encouraged them when they tried and scolded them when they failed. Jerry was the type of teacher every school should have.

In addition to teaching, he had a farm. This year he raised wheat and it was a good year for him. As we stood at the side of his field, now only stubble, he commented that this was the best place in the world. I agreed.

Early the next morning Jerry aimed me west on US 56 towards Great Bend and wished me well. In Great Bend I was not able to make any real contact with the Kiwanis Club but I tried. I did meet an old traveling friend, Kathy, the young woman riding her bicycle from Connecticut to Washington. The temperature in Kansas had been way too much for her so she took a few days rest in Nickerson and now she was once again on her way to Seattle. We exchanged big hugs and wished each other well.

Since it was early afternoon I decided to go on, heading north on US 281. The previous day had been very relaxing so I was making very good time. One of my problems when I felt good and at ease with walking my mind strayed from my trip. About five miles north of Great Bend I was supposed to turn north, but since my mind was elsewhere, I continued west and an hour later discovered that I was lost. I wasn't worried since the road was reasonably good and my trusty compass told me I was headed west. I arrived in La Crosse near dark on a Friday evening, tired but feeling great.

I entered the office of the a motel on the outskirts of La Crosse. The clerk behind the counter stood with his hands on his hips with a look of defiance on his face. A large man standing on my side of the counter yelled that he had been told he had adjoining rooms and he didn't have them. The clerk replied that he didn't have any adjoining rooms. The large man explained very loudly that the room was too small, that the shower didn't work and the television only had one channel. The volume of his voice increased with each complaint.

Finally the clerk offered to refund his money. The large man accepted, took his money and stormed out of the office. I waited a minute and calmly asked, "Do you have a room?"

The clerk looked out the window for a minute, shook his head and replied, "I do now."

I was glad my timing was good because there were no other rooms in La Crosse that night. I showered and found a place to eat. As I was waiting for my order a woman about fifty-five with far too much make-up on her small face approached my table and asked, "What year did you graduate?"

Without really thinking I said, "Forty-eight." She frowned and walked away. I was considering the reason for the question when two men, about sixty, approached and asked the same question. They too retired, unhappy with my answer.

When the waitress brought my meal I asked her why I was being asked these questions. She explained that it was the annual high school reunion in La Crosse. She also explained that all the graduating classes would be meeting tomorrow. Then she asked me, "What year did you graduate?"

I told her forty-eight and added that it was not from La Crosse. She quickly left and I noticed the level of service dropped off after my answer.

Twice during dinner I was approached with the same question. When I tried to explain that I didn't graduate from La Crosse they refused to believe me. As I was relaxing after dinner with a cup of coffee three men and a woman approached me. One overweight and balding man introduced himself as 'Red,' and then added, "I understand you graduated in '48"

I nodded and started to explain that it was from East High in Denver and not La Crosse. He ignored my explanation and introduced me to Babe. "She graduated in '48. Do you remember her?"

I considered how to answer. They wouldn't accept that I wasn't from La Crosse and they knew I had graduated in forty-eight. "Sure," I lied and turned to Babe. "Remember in History. We had that screwy teacher. She used to get mad cause we were all so dumb?"

Immediately Babe's face lit up and she sat down. She started spurting all the problems she had in high school. The overweight balding Red was apparently trying to get to know Babe a lot better, because he sat down very close to her. The two men returned to the bar and the three of us continued our reminiscing about high school. Red bought a couple rounds of drinks, which I didn't need, and then he cozied up to Babe. I was sure that my experiences in Colorado were not that different from Babe's experiences in La Crosse, Kansas. I excused myself after about thirty minutes of lying and I left. I didn't think I could have continued much longer. Red was suspicious already, but since I had shown no interest in Babe he didn't really care. I was once told that a high school reunion was a place you go and meet people who have changed so much they don't recognize you.

I slept well that night even with a guilty conscience and early the next morning, on a crystal clear day, I headed north on US 183 toward Hays, Kansas. I was feeling great and very happy with the world, though I wondered how the class reunions were going.

*****

The road to Hays was great. There was enough shoulder and very little traffic. About six miles up the road there was a small hill on the left hand side of the road. On top of the hill was an old dilapidated house with a driveway leading down to the road. The driveway was almost a half mile long. As I was looking at the house I saw an old man leave the house with a small backpack. As I reached the end of his driveway, he was sitting on a bench under an old makeshift shelter. He raised his arm and motioned me to join him. I did.

The shelter, though in need of repair, kept most of the sunshine off and the temperature was noticeably less. He handed me a bottle of water. I took a long drink. It was indeed refreshing. We talked about various things as only old men do. We agreed that, "Things aren't like they used to be." We also agreed that "Everything moves faster these days." and "There are a lot more problems in the world now than when we were young." We agreed it was hot; he had a big July Fourth party because it was his eightieth birthday. Then he opened a subject, politics, on which he had very strong opinions.

"To solve the problems in Washington, or Topeka, or any other capital is very simple. Send all those damn politicians home for two years. I know you'd have to leave someone to answer the phone, but send everyone else home. Hell, we can get along without any new laws for two years. Make them earn their living the same as the rest of us did. After they've worked for two years let them convince us on how damned valuable they really are." He expounded on his idea for over fifteen minutes. I thought it was a dumb idea at the time, but the more I thought about it, the better it sounded.

I finished his bottle of water and explained that I had to get on my way. He murmured something about young kids today not having time for a serious discussion and wished me luck. A great person!

A short time after I passed a group of dwellings called Liebenthal an attractive young lady and her daughter stopped and offered me a ride. I accepted a ride of three miles. The lady said she knew a Kiwanian in Hays and would give him a call. She did. A few miles before Hays, a member of the Kiwanis Club came out and gave me a ride to town.

He put me up in a motel, compliments of the local Kiwanis. I had a nice dinner and the next morning I headed west on what was referred to as the 'old 40.' Interstate 70 was also US 40 along here, and I was planning on following the 'old 40' that paralleled the new 40 that was Interstate 70.

The plan was probably valid, but somewhere I must have turned the wrong way. There were no 'old 40' signs to assist me and I obviously needed assistance. Somewhere between Ellis and Ogalah I found myself at the end of the road. Around two o'clock my road ended at the side of a wheat field. I hated walking back on a road, but I had no choice. I had walked about ten minutes when an old beat-up pickup truck came down the road and stopped. The driver stuck his head out the window and said, "Got yourself in a mess haven't you?"

I nodded agreement.

"Get in," he said trying to make room in his messy cab. "I saw you earlier this morning when I was driving Mommy to church." He smiled a wide friendly smile. "I'm going up toward Ponekee. I'll get you out of your mess."

It sounded good to me so I tossed my pack in the back and jumped in the front. He turned the truck around and we headed back down the road. He introduced himself as Jake and said he had to take his hog to the slaughterhouse first. I offered to help, since he had been so helpful to me. That was a mistake. We drove to his farm and lying at the side of his barn was a hog, a big hog.

Jake backed the truck up beside the hog. When I stepped from the truck, the stench hit me. It reeked of several days of fermentation in the hot Kansas sun, but that didn't seem to bother Jake. We loaded the hog with an old A frame and a 'come-along' used to raise automobile engines.

Jake was an interesting individual. He had graduated from college and apparently worked for either the city or county in some capacity. He explained that he didn't like city living. He wanted to know his neighbors and he wanted them to know him. After the day with the hog, I was certain his neighbors knew him. He was on his way to Ponekee to help a friend with his harvest. It was important to Jake that he help his neighbors.

The truck was almost as interesting as Jake. It was an old Ford, about 1950 I guessed. Jake had not cleaned out the cab for several years. There were numerous containers from fast food restaurants on the floor along with various Pepsi and Coke cans, bottles and cups on the floor, in the glove compartment that wouldn't close, and on the dashboard.

The slaughter house was a large compound with a chain link fence around it. The gate was closed. Jake drove up to the front gate and stopped. We got out and dumped the hog directly in front of the front gate. "They'll know what to do with it." I imagined they would.

After we dropped the hog off I was beginning to be concerned. My pack had been in the back of that truck with that stinking hog. I wondered if I was going to have to put up with that odor for the rest of my trip.

Jake asked me where I wanted to get out. I really didn't know. I was lost and I had no idea what road I was on. I rode with Jake for about twenty minutes. Some was westerly, some was easterly and some was northerly. I saw a wide spot in the road ahead and suggested that would be fine. Jake pulled over and I got my pack out and thanked him.

I started down the road, heading west. Jake turned around and went back the direction we had come. My pack did not have any odor about it that I could notice, but I wasn't sure. I headed west on my road. I did not know what road it was but I knew it was not a US highway. There were no shoulders, but there was no traffic either so I just headed west. I came to a stop sign and a better road headed north so I took that.

*****

As evening approached, I was thinking about a place to sleep. I was not worried because I had plenty of water and food, but I was concerned. I headed down a long hill. At the bottom of the hill was a bridge. It was past seven and I was tired. I decided to sleep under the bridge. There was a path from the road down under the bridge. I took it without hesitation and entered the shade under the bridge.

It was cool and welcomed. I waited a minute for my eyes to adjust to the dimness. Immediately I found that I was not alone. There were three others under the bridge, and it appeared that they had been there for quite some time.

I felt that I had entered someone's home, uninvited. I was very uncomfortable. A man about fifty slid down the small hill to where I stood and said, "Welcome." He was dirty, unshaven and had long scraggly hair, but he also had a smile and a warm handshake. He introduced himself as George, helped me take my pack off and invited me up the trail to his place. I accepted.

Perhaps I should have been concerned about my safety, but I wasn't. George explained that he and his family, a woman and a man both about thirty, were homeless. George had been fired from a job in Topeka and they were on their way to Denver. He had family there and all would be well.

That evening I shared their dry bread and Spam, and they shared my Twinkies and Pepsi. George was excited about an old man walking across the country and I was concerned about the three of them with no place to live. I did not sleep well that night. I was not concerned about protection from my new found friends under the bridge. I was concerned that in our world there were many who slipped through the cracks and were lost as productive helpful individuals. I believed strongly in capitalism, but I also believed in caring. I hoped that the two were not mutually exclusive.

The next morning I emptied two of my three water containers into their tank, thanked them for their company and headed west. Another hard, hot day on the west Kansas plains.

*****

It had been a long hard day of walking, and I arrived in Hoxie, Kansas, around four o'clock in the afternoon. I say 'about' because I did not have a watch. I had lost one watch a few days out of New York City and another halfway through Pennsylvania so I decided I did not need a watch. Time was no longer important to me and losing watches was a

Freudian problem. I was tired so I decided to find a motel, go to bed early and that would allow me to get an early start tomorrow. I looked at the map and decided I could make Colby, Kansas, tomorrow, some thirty-six miles ahead.

I found me a cheap motel, showered, went out to eat and went to bed early. I was very tired.

When I travel I am often concerned about being caught in a fire. I am sure it relates back to some class B movie I saw as a kid. Fires in strange places bother me. The motel room I had was on the ground floor and there were no obstructions to interfere with a quick exit. I went to sleep quickly.

Sometime just before morning I was awakened by someone pounding on my door. I was convinced that the motel was on fire, and I sure did not want to die in a fire in a strange town. So I jumped up and ran out the door as fast as I could. I ran into the parking lot and turned around to watch the flames streaking into the sky above.

There was no fire. It was not the middle of the night The sun was up and it was hot. It was afternoon. The noise I had heard was the housekeeper trying to awaken me to ask if I was going to stay over another night. I had slept almost twenty hours. I was embarrassed. Partially of my embarrassment was because I had thought there was a fire and rushed out of my room. However, most of my chagrin was because I had no clothes. I sleep in the nude. I was an old man standing naked in the middle of the parking lot on a hot Kansas afternoon. There were ten or twelve tourists and maids wondering why I was so excited.

A couple of the ladies were in their sixties and their mouths were literally wide open. An old man, about my age, smiled widely and two of the maids covered their mouths with their hands for some reason. They were in shock.

I was going to tell them that I didn't want to die in a fire. Instead I told the maid, "Yes, I'll stay over another night." And I walked back to my room with as much confidence as I could. It was difficult to have 'dignity' with my hands covering what little I had to cover, and chagrin on my face.

Later when I went to the office to sign up for another night, the lady who owned the motel had a big smile on her face, but she did not say anything. I asked her to please apologize to the maid and she said that I had made this day a big day for everyone in the motel. I had created more excitement than they normally have all year long. She still charged me for my room.

I slept very well that night, wearing a clean pair of my shorts, and I left early the next morning, long before anyone at the motel was concerned about my staying over another night. I did not want to talk to them about my stupidity, nudity or anything else.

In Colby I got a motel room, took a shower and relaxed. One of my major problems was my pack. It was not designed for heavy, constant use. The canvas would tear. I would get it sewed up and it would tear someplace else. I lost some minor items because of the tears. The aluminum frame held up very well, but my PVC sign frame gave me a few problems. Now my pack needed to be repaired; I took it to a shoe repair shop and they fixed it. Early Tuesday morning I headed out for Goodland.

*****

I left Colby about three in the morning. That was a mistake. Between three-thirty and five-thirty I was visited by three law enforcement officers, a sheriff, a Marshall and a highway patrolman. I figured someone drove by, called 9-1-1 and told them there was some old man out there on the road. At that time of the day, they had nothing to do so they came out to see that old man. None of them harassed me or suggested that I shouldn't be there. The Marshall probably asked the question more directly than any of the others, "What the hell are you doing?" I explained what I was doing to each of the officers and they individually went on their merry way, but I sure wasted a lot of time. On the other hand, the sunrise on the plains that morning was sensational.

I sat down and leaned my pack against a telephone pole, and for almost an hour I watched the eastern sky lighten. It was a conscious decision on my part to relax. I reminded myself that I was here to enjoy the trip, not just get home and tell about it, but to become a part of this country. I sat, with my back to California, watching the sun rise. I thought of all those before me who had relaxed on these plains and watched the sun rise. The Native Americans for hundreds or perhaps thousands of years had been here. The mountain men, the settlers crossing the plains in the nineteenth century, the railroad builders, the cowboys, the farmers had all seen it. The families in the 1930's heading for California had watched the same sun rise. I thought about the servicemen in both world wars, and in Korea and Viet Nam who crossed here heading for their ports and their ships.

Many had seen it before, I knew that, but I was seeing it now. I relaxed and carefully set each item in my memory, to recall in days hence when I was in need of solace.

There were several clouds that morning in the eastern sky. There were streaks across the sky to the north tinged with red. Overhead the streaks were gray. To the side I could see the cars and trucks on the Interstate, but I had to listen very carefully to hear them. To one side there were two radio towers, blinking their presence to all. The clouds in the sky over Colby, now ten miles back, were lighted from the city. There were three farm houses on the skyline. Each had turned on their lights.

I heard the birds and insects. At first they were only sporadic, but as the light increased so did their presence. As dawn approached the cries of the insects gave way to the songs of the birds. A fox darted across the road returning from a night of hunting and probably feeding. It was a beautiful morning. I was glad to be alive and I was glad I was walking across the United States. But I could only sit so long. As the first of the sun shown bright red in the eastern sky I decided that I had to be on my way home. I slowly picked up my pack, slung it on my back and headed into the west where it was still black.

The road from Colby to Goodland was close to ideal. It was a good road parallel to an Interstate. That meant very little traffic on an acceptable road.

In Edson, in the middle of a hot afternoon, a member of the Goodland Kiwanis Club, Bob Dall, came out to rescue me. Bob was expecting a young man about thirty with a beard. He was very surprised to find an old man almost sixty, well shaven. Luckily Bob recognized me from the sign on the back of my pack

In Goodland he assured me I would have a place to stay for the night with a fellow Kiwanian. He then drove me around Goodland and introduced me to his friends, and his city. He also arranged for a radio interview and a newspaper interview. Both went very well. Leaving the radio station we bumped into a candidate for governor of Kansas. He introduced himself, "Phelps, and I'm running for Governor." And he was, running in tennis shoes across the state. He showed considerable interest in my walking across the state until he found out that I was not a Kansan and he changed his attention to Bob Dall. When Bob introduced himself, Phelps thought he said 'Dole,' and showed considerable attention until my guide pointed out that the spelling of his name was different.

It was in Goodland that I bought a new pair of shoes. At the beginning I had four pairs broken in, four different brands. Yvonne mailed me one pair to Nevada, Missouri, and there was still a pair at home. But I needed a pair now. The last pair had dissolved too quickly. When it came time to buy another pair of shoes, I chose Rockports. I had not received the backing from Rockport that I wanted, but Rockport had the best shoes for me for the walking I was doing.

Goodland was also a step for me as far as time zones. As I came into Goodland I was in Mountain Daylight Savings time, one hour from the time zone in California.

It was confusing to hear anyone give the time. "Our meeting begins at twelve, local time. That's eleven where you are so I'll pick you up at ten, your time, but here that's eleven." The next day, in St. Francis, I would be back on Central Daylight Savings Time. It is interesting how we can develop ways to confuse ourselves so easily. The time zones were not as exciting to me as the idea that soon I would be seeing the Rocky Mountains on the horizon.

*****

The land was now flat, very flat. The rolling hills of the east were gone. Irrigated fields were common. This irrigation was not irrigation as practiced in northern California with canals and dikes and water flowing in rows. The irrigation here was in circular sprays. The circle was about a mile in diameter with a radial arm circling the field very slowly. There were as many as twelve sets of wheels and water in large amounts pumped from deep underground and sprayed across the field. The drive for the wheels was computer controlled and the radial line of sprayers appeared perfectly straight. I thought about the computer program to keep the line straight, but decided it was not that sophisticated. I did know that a lot of water was being drawn from the ground at several points across that part of Kansas. I wondered if it was being replaced. I knew it wasn't.

As I walked across the last part of Kansas, I found that I was thinking a great deal about the finish of the trip, walking down the two days from Sonora Pass to my town of Sonora. I knew I would go on to San Francisco. I also thought about the last two days as I would be walking up the San Francisco peninsula, completing the four-month journey. I was concerned that I might be so run down that I would only be moving at about one and a half miles an hour.

On the roads of Kansas during the first weeks of July were several custom harvesters. They were moving north to harvest the vast wheat lands of Nebraska, having already completed most of the fields of

Kansas. Each tribe of custom harvesters amounted to a couple of big harvesting machines on flatbed trucks, a truck with maintenance and repair equipment, a couple of pickups and a large motor home or camper trailer. They moved from Texas north across the mid continent to harvest the crops. It was a great summer job for those who endured, and a great money maker for those with the harvesters, most of the time.

This summer, however, the custom harvesters were having problems. They explained to me, at a rest stop near Great Bend, that it rained a lot in Kansas when it should have been dry. The crews sat around doing nothing but collecting pay. Then it became hot, very hot, and all the wheat in Kansas matured at the same time. There was too much for the harvesters to do and not enough time. The bosses had to make decisions on which farms they harvested and which they left to waste away. Now the harvest-time was over in Kansas and they were headed to Nebraska and north. As they moved along the roads they were a big caravan, a caravan that often took up the entire road. Many times I had to stop and let the caravan pass. They did not move over for me and they were a lot wider than eight feet. I did not argue with them.

I was resting just north of the county line in the shade of the only tree in that part of Kansas. I had been walking for about seven hours into a headwind and I was tired. A large van pulled up and the driver, a woman in her fifties, stuck her head out the window and said, "You look mighty hot."

I slowly got up and approached the van. I said, "Good afternoon, ladies. I hope you have some cool water." I introduced myself and they smiled back and looked at each other.

Finally the driver said, "I'm Betty Mae from St. Francis. Bob Dall told me you were coming and I just thought you might need some help."

"Do you mean to tell me," I said, "that you two ladies drove all the way from St. Francis just to see if I needed help?" We were about three miles from St. Francis.

They nodded, invited me into their air conditioned van and asked if I had enough for the day. I said I had. I had covered over twenty-five miles in hundred degree temperature with a headwind. I had had enough.

Betty Mae and her friend drove me back to St Francis and introduced me to most of the people in town. At least they introduced me to all the important people. I had a newspaper interview and met several people at the power plant, where Betty Mae's husband worked. I was introduced to everyone at the cafe, at the library and at the church. The two people that I will remember forever were Judy and Ralph.

Judy was an exciting young lady of sixty who spent her winters as a sorority mother in Boulder and her summers as cultural head of St. Francis. Her enthusiasm for life flowed from every word and her love of everyone was obvious when she spoke. Judy was known locally as the 'hat' lady. Her home had over a thousand hats. She said she had one just for me, but she couldn't find it. I will always wonder what it would have looked like. She is a very alive person. I hope to see her again.

Ralph was eighty-four, lived in a small house at the edge of town, and created artistic masterpieces from discarded metal. He had several sculptures in his museum at the side of his house, but his real masterpieces were well outside town on a lonely road. Betty Mae, Ralph, and a couple friends, drove me out to a lonely spot on the Cherry River. There Ralph had fabricated life-size silhouettes of a buffalo, a mounted Indian with headdress, a jack rabbit and a beaver. All were from the metal bottoms of old discarded water tanks, quarter-inch steel plate.

The Indian was on a hill overlooking the road. The buffalo, rabbit and beaver were near the road at a site near where the last buffalo was killed about a hundred years ago. Below this sight was the Cherry River. As we were admiring the sculptures, Ralph commented, "Isn't this the most beautiful place in the world."

I had heard this said before on this long walk home, and I would hear it some more. But Ralph said it with more devotion than anyone else. Ralph believed it stronger than anyone else. I agreed with him. I would never have thought that I would see anything in northeastern Kansas that I would feel that way about, but Ralph convinced me.

I spent Wednesday night with Betty Mae and her husband in their home in St. Francis. Early the next morning she fed me a good breakfast, drove me a couple miles from town and sent me on my way. A few miles later Ralph came by and we talked some more. Ralph represented to me the strength that some older people earn through life. He drove me to the Colorado border, turned his car around and waved good-bye.

My memories of Kansas were warm and hot. I have warm feeling because of the people I had met. All of the people, beginning with John and Lucy and ending with Betty Mae, Judy and Ralph, warmed my heart and made me feel proud to have met them. I also had some very hot days in Kansas, hot, and many times very humid.

I had spent more time in Kansas than in any other state, but I was also more welcomed there. The roads were cleaner and, toward the end, straighter. I enjoyed Kansas, but now I was headed for Colorado, my home state, my sister and her family, and memories of long ago.

Colorado

Colorado

When I had entered Kansas two weeks ago the temperature had increased at least ten degrees. Now as I was leaving Kansas the temperature dropped ten degrees. Colorado was cooler and the road had larger shoulders that added to my walking comfort.

I was born in Craig, Colorado, almost sixty years ago. Craig, located in the northwest corner of the state, was where I spent most of my first twenty years. I had lots of memories here, both good and bad. When I was thirteen my father died of a heart attack. One year later my mother died of another heart attack. Jo, my older sister, had just turned twenty-one when Mom died so my little sister and I moved in with her. On this trip I planned to visit Jo in Grand Junction and see some of her children in Denver within the week. Colorado was an emotional paradox for me. I wanted to see and visit my early surroundings, but I knew there would be emotional requirements I wasn't sure I wanted to meet. I had no choice now. I was on my long walk home and I was headed into Colorado.

I headed west on US 36 into Colorado and the road was straight and flat. Two of the next three days there was not a bend in the road. From Joes it took me one day to Anton and another day to a night in the middle of nowhere and finally the next day to Strasburg.

Just before Strasburg was Byers. As I was having lunch in Byers I met a couple from Missouri, Ed and Mary Lou. They were absentee landlords with 145 acres of wheat nearby. They were here to arrange for the harvesting of their wheat by a custom harvest crew from Canada. I invited myself along when Ed said he was going out to see how his harvesters were doing and he took me out to his field. Before the day had ended I rode one path around the field in a huge harvester with one of the workers on the custom crew. I also went down to the silo with Ed and watched the operation. In addition to weighing the wheat, the weigh master determined the moisture content and the protein content of the wheat. The price received depended upon these characteristics, so Ed watched very carefully.

Late that day Ed took me back to the Strasburg Inn Hotel, where I was staying. The Strasburg Inn Hotel was a European style hotel in a very American style town. It was operated by five very kind and very generous people. They grew most of their own food, and raised chickens for eggs and goats for their milk. They lived a frugal communal life, but they seemed to enjoy it.

It was strange because no one else I met in Strasburg even knew about the hotel. It was the best kept secret in Strasburg. I enjoyed it because I don't like fancy places because you pay for too much show. I didn't need show.

*****

From Strasburg, on Monday, I headed west. During a break at about eight thirty on Monday morning I saw the Rocky Mountains. My first goal had been the Appalachian Mountains, then the Ohio River, then the Mississippi River, now the sight of the Rocky Mountains excited me. The next goal, only a week away, was the top of the Rocky Mountains.

I made it to Bennett well before lunch. I had intended to head north to Prospect Valley, but after talking to people in Bennett I decided to proceed west to Watkins. There was too much truck traffic on the narrow road to Prospect Valley and she couldn't recall any motel there. Since the road west had practically no traffic, I headed west. I made it easily to Watkins, a glorified truck stop, which was very unfriendly to a walking old man. It bothered me when they wouldn't let me bring my pack into a restaurant. I found a small cafe that allowed me to bring my pack inside.

There were storm clouds in the western sky and I didn't want to continue further. I found a motel and that evening I called my nephew, Paul, in Denver. I had not seen Paul, my sister Jo's son, for over thirty years and I wondered what he might be like. I knew he was wondering about his uncle, the one he always called, 'Unc.'

The next day I headed into Denver on East Colfax. The hospital where Dad died was on East Colfax. My Aunt Nonnie and Uncle Al lived just off East Colfax and I was in their kitchen when my mother died. I went to a theater to see a film in Spanish and afterward trying to speak Spanish with a beautiful sixteen year old señorita. I wandered where she was now. I had graduated from East High School in Denver back in 1948 which was on East Colfax. There were street cars on East Colfax in 1948. There were lots of memories lingering along the road.

Shortly after lunch I called Paul and told him where I would be waiting. I remembered Paul as a very vocal and gregarious young man. I was surprised when this bearded, heavy set, forty year old with two dogs came up and said, "Hi, 'Unc.'" I may have been surprised, but tears came to my eyes as I hugged my nephew.

That evening I had dinner with Paul and two of his sisters, my nieces, at a Chinese restaurant in downtown Denver. Liz, whom I remembered as a very energetic blonde brat, was now a beautiful, exciting, blonde woman. And little Laurie, whom I couldn't even remember was still little, but very beautiful and loving.

I have been married almost thirty-three years and during that time I had seen Paul and Liz twice and Laura only once. Our family did not have close ties, so the evening with 'family' was important to me. We talked for hours.

Paul was a master tool and die maker with a local company and he enjoyed his job. He never married and I doubted that he ever would. He enjoyed working with machines rather than people. Machines responded in a predetermined fashion, unlike people. He loved his two dogs and would not be able to find any woman who would give him the devotion he received from his dogs. He was very open about his thoughts, too frank for many.

Liz was a self-employed psychotherapist trying to expand into rolfing and yet survive in Boulder. She lived frugally in a mobile home, but she appeared to enjoy life considerably. Like her brother, Liz had never been married, and didn't seem to worry much about it, a healthy sign.

Laura was a nurse working at an AIDS center at Denver General Hospital. She had to put up with death as a common denominator in all her efforts. That must have been difficult. Though she was physically very small, she was very strong emotionally. I admired her tremendously.

All three of them were beautiful in the very broad sense of the word. Their parents had been divorced when they were young, but they showed no animosity toward life. Spending time with them was an important and very personal part of my walk. My walk now was shared with family members from my past. Seeing my nieces and a nephew increased my enjoyment of my walk. But it made me homesick for my family. I wanted to hold my wife and tell her how important she was. I wanted to see my daughters and hear their problems, listen to their dreams and tell them I loved them. Old men should not get homesick, but I was

After the dinner in Denver I spent the night at Laura's house because Paul was ashamed of his housekeeping and wouldn't allow me in his home. Laura and I sat up for several hours talking. She was a wonderful and very strong woman, too strong for most men.

The next morning Paul picked me up and he showed me through the place where he worked. Paul seems to command a great deal of respect from those I met. I enjoyed the tour. After we left his factory we drove to Boulder to see Liz and we tried to find another niece. My brother's daughter, Lynn, was at work, but we couldn't find where, and we couldn't find the address we had from the phone book. The numbers and street names on the outskirts of Boulder were not very complete. We were unsuccessful, but we tried.

Paul, Liz and I talked for a while during the afternoon and then Paul took me to Greeley and sent me on my way. It was nice to meet family that I didn't really know. I was glad I could be proud of them. They were fine people and I was very glad to have met them again. I hope that we will become a little closer in the future.

*****

But now it was time for me to get back on my long walk home. In Greeley I called Robert. He had written me a letter that I picked up in Nevada, Missouri, inviting me to visit him. I was glad I did. I stayed the night with Robert and his wife in a very comfortable and big house. His wife helped a great deal by washing all my clothes.

The entertainment that evening was Robert and the starlings. Behind their house they had a large tree and in the evenings several hundred, or, according to Robert, thousands, of starlings headed into the tree to roost for the night. Robert did not support this because many of them roosted over his patio. If he allowed them to stay, his patio became a mess, a big stinking mess. So throughout the evening about every fifteen to twenty minutes Robert got up, took a big metal pot and a large wooden spoon and stepped out onto the patio and pounded the drum. The starlings would leave and Robert would return with a victorious smile on his face. Jo Ann would just smile.

The next morning I headed up the road to Loveland. I stayed in a motel, compliments of the Loveland Kiwanis. Loveland appeared to be a very beautiful town. In the center of the city is a big lake that adds considerably to the city's beauty. I left a seven o'clock call because I had a breakfast appointment. I did not get the call, but then my seven o'clock appointment didn't arrive at seven either. Colorado had not changed. I went to breakfast around eight with Leo, a Kiwanian from Loveland and he showed me around the city some more. It was interesting that the highlights to Leo, a lawyer about my age, were the civic buildings and the home the city had built for the seniors. Later I went to the Post Office to pick up my mail. I got my fifth pair of shoes that day. It was again enjoyable to hear that all was well back in Sonora. I spent a long time reading the letter from my wife. Sonora was a long ways away, and I wanted to be home.

Walking up the eastern side of the Rocky Mountains was a wet and tiring experience. The day was rainy and cold as I headed up the mountain. I had two garbage bags. I put one over my body with a cut so my head would stick out. I put another garbage bag over my pack. I was convinced that they were as good as any rain gear I had seen, and they were cheaper too. The road up Big Thompson Canyon was narrow and the visibility was not great with the heavy rain so when I came to a wide spot in the road I stopped. I was sitting under a large tree admiring the green trees and gray sky as a large truck pulled into the same wide spot. When it groaned to a stop I recognized it as a garbage truck. Only garbage trucks made that guttural, groaning sound as they stop. Apparently it was built into them. They sounded the same all across the country. The young, blonde haired driver stuck his head out of the window and asked, "Want a ride?"

Sitting on a rock in a garbage bag with my pack also covered with a garbage bag I asked, "In the front or the back?"

"In the front." He responded with a big smile. I asked him how far to town and he said it was over five miles. I thanked him kindly and explained that I was not suffering and I would continue on my way on foot. He shook his head and left and I did too. I knew I would be in Estes Park long before dark.

Just after I entered the city of Estes Park, Dave, a Kiwanian, picked me up and took me to his house to dry out. Later that evening Dave, his wife and I went out to dinner and they showed me around Estes Park. Estes Park was a tourist trap of the first order. I was reminded of Lancaster, Pennsylvania. I was also reminded of my home town of Sonora, but Sonora was a lot smaller than Estes Park.

I went to bed early and the next morning Dave and I went to the local McDonalds where we met Leo and some of his friends. The morning was wet, cold and foggy and they were concerned about my walking across Trail Ridge. Dave drove me to a spot just inside Rocky Mountain National Park. I assured him I could make it from there so he let me out of his car. Today I would cross the Rocky Mountains. The road, Trail Ridge, was twelve miles above ten thousand feet. By the end of the day, I was willing to believe it.

I headed up US 34 to Trail Ridge. Several people had suggested that there were easier places to cross the Rockies than Trail Ridge. I agreed, but since I only intended to take this walk once, I was going over the top. This was very impressive to those who do not backpack. I was certain the altitude would not present me with a problem. It didn't and neither did the long uphill grade. The rise was about a seven percent grade, steeper than most passes, but not at all steep to a backpacker. By this time in my walk I was in excellent shape, and the day was cool, so I headed up Trail Ridge at my usual three to three and half miles per hour.

As I climbed steadily up the mountain the fog from below would often sweep up and envelop me for several minutes. I was walking in a cloud. The heavy wisps of moisture laden air swirled about me. It was cooling and welcome. Then the cloud would evaporate and the sun would shine down. I could see the cloud now below me grasping for a hold in the ravines below. The tall pines pushing through the cloud and up to the sky. Across the large canyon and on the next mountain, a mile away, I could see my road winding to the top of Trail Ridge. Then the clouds would again blow up the mountain and envelop me. This happened several times as I climbed. It was a cool and beautiful day to climb a mountain.

It was now Saturday and the weekend traffic was very heavy. Many of the cars going up honked and often as I walked by a 'Scenic Turnout' several tourists would talk with me. As I approached the last few miles shortly after two, the uphill traffic was at a standstill and I was passing the same motorists who had honked at me earlier.

I had talked to a ranger earlier and he had explained to me the location of the top of Trail Ridge. "It is not marked, but the road goes down to the Visitor Center on the other side. You won't miss it."

I didn't miss it. I was anticipating it and when I reached the top I had tears in my eyes and a lump in my throat. That didn't stop me from forcing my fist into the air and letting loose a gigantic, enormous yell.

The cars, now stopped because of the heavy traffic, sounded their horns and several people, mostly young, rushed from their cars and came over and gave me hugs and kisses. I was physically as high as I would get, and I was also emotionally very high.

Just then there was a bright flash of lightning and a simultaneous loud clap of thunder. Hail began to fall immediately and everyone returned to their cars. Since my sign and frame could offer me cover, I flipped the sign over my head and watched the hail and rain fall. I also felt the satisfaction of being there. Later, when I told a friend about the lightning and thunder, she suggested it was Nature's way of informing me that Nature was more powerful than I. I had never questioned that Nature was much more powerful than I, but I wasn't sure that the lightning and thunder proved it.

I walked the last mile to the Visitor's Center near the top and had an enormous spaghetti dinner. I had intended to spend the night at the top, but found that was not possible. I knew I could sneak into a gully somewhere and no one would notice me. I also knew how sensitive the tundra was. I could not allow myself to do that. I would just continue on down to Grand Lake.

As I walked out of the restaurant I again saw my young bicyclist from Connecticut, Kathy. This was the third time we had met. Fate and circumstances had brought us together again. We hugged and exchanged some experiences. She was biking down to Grand Lake and she told me I could find a night's lodging at the Youth Hostel in Grand Lake. I immediately headed down the mountain.

My pace had quickened to just over four miles per hour. It was down hill, cool, and I was in a hurry. At shortly after eight that evening I entered Grand Lake, thanks to a short ride from a lonely tourist. I was very tired physically, but still very high emotionally. Now I had a new problem; there was no room at the inn.

Grand Lake was celebrating Buffalo Days and the place was crowded. No room at the inn! Finally Kathy and a friend let me share their room. They had no beds so we all slept on the floor with our pads and sleeping bags. I didn't want to sleep out that night, because it was going to be very wet. I appreciated the offer from Kathy.

I sat on a patio with Kathy and her friend to watch the fireworks on the lake. It occurred to me that I had achieved another goal. I had crossed the Rocky Mountains. The water here flowed west. I was getting closer to home. The ZIP codes had increased from 07083 to 80517. The radio stations now began with the letter 'K' instead of 'W' and I was only one time zone away from Sonora.

I was tired and my muscles were very sore from the exceptionally long walk across the mountains, but I awoke very early Sunday morning and couldn't go back to sleep. I got up quietly, left a note for Kathy and escaped into the bright morning sun. I had an enormous breakfast and headed west again.

I reached the junction of US 40 about noon and debated going east to Granby for the night, only about a mile, or going on to Hot Sulphur Springs, ten miles west. Most of the pain from the morning was hidden under my second set of Tylenol Gel Caps so I headed west.

I was glad I did because in Hot Sulphur Springs I met the owner and manager of the Riverside Hotel, Abraham Rodriguez. Abraham owned, managed, bartended, cooked, registered, changed beds, served and told old jokes at the Riverside Hotel. He had no employees. I got there on

Sunday, but the previous night he had all thirty-one rooms full, cooked and served fifty-six meals and had a healthy bar trade.

The Riverside Hotel was a European style hotel with small rooms, most with a sink, and a shared bath. The one difference this hotel had from any I have stayed in before was that the rooms all had women's names instead of numbers. I stayed in Mae's room, overlooking the Colorado River.

The next morning I awoke early and had a hot cup of coffee. Abraham complained that he had lived there for almost ten years and he still had not met any interesting or exciting women. As hard as he worked, he would never have a chance to meet one anyway. I think every female knew he was looking for someone to work as hard as he was. No one would volunteer for that.

I headed west through Byers Canyon, a narrow canyon with the highway on one side of the Colorado River and a railroad on the other. I relaxed often to enjoy the views, steep granite cliffs, rushing water and a beautiful blue sky. The sky became more threatening as I headed on down the Colorado River to Kremmling. I arrived there about noon. During the afternoon the sky was heavily clouded and there were bolts of lightning visible in the nearby mountains. I talked with the Ranger at the Forest Service in Kremmling and was told there was no place, absolutely no place, to camp between Kremmling and Steamboat Springs, not even a large culvert. Steamboat Springs was fifty-two miles away.

I considered my alternatives. If I stayed in Kremmling I could start early the next morning and make it to Steamboat Springs late the next day. Or I could start out now, get as far as I could, find some shelter for the night and then finish the next day in Steamboat Springs.

I discussed these alternatives with the Ranger and he said I only had one real alternative: take the bus. The weather at eight thousand feet and above was harsh, rain was expected, and I shouldn't camp where it was not allowed.

I decided that I knew best so I started walking west toward Steamboat Springs. I was about four or five miles from town when it started sprinkling and the clouds seemed to descend. There was no shelter anyplace. Deciding that I should reconsider, I returned to Kremmling. By the time I got there it was pouring and I was wet.

I caught the bus to Steamboat Springs. I was glad I did, because the Kiwanis Club of Steamboat Springs met the night I got there. When I arrived at the bus station I called Cliff and he came over to pick me up immediately.

I attended the Kiwanis meeting Monday evening and spent the night in Cliff's home. Cliff and his wife were an energetic couple in their late fifties. She had spent the day on a ten mile hike to a mountain lake for lunch. Both were in excellent condition and both enjoyed life enormously.

Steamboat Springs had grown significantly from what I remembered from forty-five years before. I was given one interesting and unusual statistic about Steamboat Springs. It had twelve thousand pillows. I had never heard of population or housing referred to by number of pillows. Actually it made sense. The town had room for twelve thousand people, in the correct increments. I also was told that the Japanese owned a large part of the operation there. The purchase was over ten years ago, but no one seemed upset about it. No one had lost their jobs either.

It was a comfortable evening and a quiet night. Early Tuesday morning Cliff drove me two miles west of town and sent me on my way. I had forty miles to cover to get to Craig. During the day I accepted two rides of three miles each. The highway, US 40, was narrow and the shoulders were narrow or nonexistent. There was a lot of traffic early in the day, mostly people on their way to work in Steamboat Springs. The living in Steamboat had become too expensive for many, so they lived in the outlying areas and commuted to work.

*****

The road toward Craig was alongside the Yampa River. I saw lots of wild animals, mostly deer and significant numbers of wild geese, redwing blackbirds and several hawks. The hills had pine trees and sagebrush, a strange combination, but common at this elevation. During the day three storm clouds dumped their cargo on me. I had hail twice and rain once. The biggest problem I had was the moisture stirred up as the cars and trucks came by. The moisture cooled the air, but it also increased the weight of my pack.

I approached Craig about five o'clock on Tuesday evening. As I came closer to Craig, I saw many views that I recalled from earlier, much earlier times. The road had changed its location in most places, but I could usually see where it had been. I saw many houses that seemed familiar, but I was not certain. I recognized hills where I had hunted jackrabbits with my old single shot twenty-two.

Craig had changed from when I was a boy. The population when I left forty-five years ago was something less than 2000. At the end of the war it boomed, with oil exploration and refining, to about 7000, then died again to around 4000. Then in the eighties it grew to over 16,000 with the oil shale boom and the construction of the coal fired electric generation plant. With oil shale being shunned and construction of the electric plant complete Craig dropped to its present population of around 6000. The boom and bust had been hard on the town.

As I sat on top of a hill where I could see Craig below, a small storm, part hail and part rain, was taking place. I pulled to the side of the road and considered what I was going to do in Craig. I wanted to see the house where I was born and the steep hill behind it where we used to sled. I wanted to see the garage where I spent many hours with Dad and Mom. I wanted to see some of my old schoolmates.

I wrote down the names of my schoolmates, so I would not forget them. Charlene Jones—my first true love because we had played house together when we were six. I remembered her as a kind and generous person. Herbie Foster—we used to hunt jackrabbits on the hill above our house. He was a better shot than I was. Herbie lived only a block away. Jimmy Newell—Jimmy was a close friend to me. We spent many afternoons fishing on the Yampa River only a mile south of my home. Jimmy was gentle and caring. Joe Stoddard—he was my competition both in sports and in the class room. He always did better than me in sports, but I could best him in the classroom, most of the time. With the names written down so I knew I would remember them, I entered Craig.

Another summer storm was making itself felt in Craig. I remembered these storms as cool, exciting and something to break the activities of the day. Now they were more of a burden associated with the mountain climate.

I walked down the main streets of Craig and my memories were weighing heavy on my thoughts. I was recalling things I had not thought about for forty-five years. Little things like the grocery store that was kitty corner from Dad's garage, Smith's Grocery. Just before the war a car had crashed into the corner where Mr. Smith had his vegetables. He boarded up the windows with plywood since winter was coming. He said next year he would get new windows and new vegetable bins.

The war came and Mr. Smith left the plywood windows and delayed buying his vegetable bins. He was always 'a gonna' fix them up, "with those new white enamel bins and little sprayers that go psst and keep everything fresh."

When Mom died in 1945 and we left Craig, Mr. Smith still had plywood in his windows and was still 'a gonna' fix them. I guess it was like

Colorado, they are always 'a gonna.' Maybe someday they will, but I hope not.

I found out that all my friends that I wanted to see in Craig were still there. They had not moved away. They were still there, buried in Craig. They had all died. Charlene had cancer. Herbie was killed in an auto accident. Jimmie died of asphyxiation on a hunting trip, and Joe died of something that they could not recall a few years before. These were all friends of mine, the same age as I was and they were all dead.

I was very depressed. I spent that night in a motel, but I slept very little. The emotional highs I had had in Denver and on Trail Ridge were now countered with a deep emotional low. It seemed wrong that I should be enjoying such a great adventure while they could enjoy nothing, yet they were the same age as I. They were dead.

I found Delores, who had been our housekeeper for the last few years before my parents died. Since Mom and Dad both worked, Delores cooked many of our meals and kept the house clean. A lot of my teaching at home came from Delores. Frank, Delores's husband, worked at the garage and I remembered both as fine people. Frank had died and Delores had remarried and owned a flower shop in Craig.

Early Wednesday morning I stopped by the flower shop and Delores was very excited. We talked for a couple hours, but I had some things I had to do. I had to visit my parents' graves. I assured Delores I would see her the next day and spend the night with her before I left.

I stopped by the funeral home and asked about my parents graves. I needed to know where they were. One of the men there looked up the information in a big thick book and offered to take me out to the grave site. I accepted and we drove out to the cemetery.

I remembered as a young boy that the cemetery was a long way from town It was over the creek, past our house, up a big hill to the big cemetery on top. The roads he used were not there when I was young. The bridge we crossed was not there when I was young. The distance was much shorter than I remembered but it was the same cemetery.

I looked at the graves of my parents for a few minutes with tears in my eyes. I returned to the pickup and he took me back to town. I thanked him and walked around town for a while

I spent the night with Joe Edwards and his wife. Joe had worked for Dad at the garage and he remembered me well, but I could not recall him. The next morning Joe drove me around town for over two hours. The Mattingly Garage that I remembered as a huge complex was now a small parking lot with a 'For Sale' sign on the corner of it. Our house, which I knew would be there forever, was gone and replaced by a Gofer Mini Mart. I noticed the beer coolers were directly above where our cesspool had been. The one encouraging thing was that the hill behind our house, which I remembered as steep for sled riding, was still steep.

I thanked Joe for his help and walked back to the cemetery. There were the graves, the graves of my parents and also Charlene, Herbie, Jimmy and Joe. I pondered death and dying, but I also thought about life. I had no answers, but I had lots of questions.

I returned to Craig and to Delores's house for the night. She was still a grand person who grossly over served and expected me to eat all that she cooked. I did my best. We talked far into the night about my parents, my siblings and our friends. She recalled many stories of my parents that I had never heard before, or if I had, I had forgotten them. It was encouraging to know that Delores loved my parents as much as I did. Their death was a big blow to her too. It made me feel good knowing how great my parents were in her eyes.

I went to bed, but slept very little, too many memories in too little space. My mind was unsettled. Early the next morning Delores again fed me well and I went on my way. Craig had been an abstract, confused memory before my trip. Now it was more concrete but still more than a little confused.

I now had a friend in Craig. Delores was far more than just a friend, she was someone who had a big role in my growth, and it had been a caring role. Craig was also different from anywhere else I had been. In Craig a local telephone call was only a dime and there was only four digits. It had gone boom and bust so many times. If someone came in and promised the moon, they wouldn't believe it. I do not blame them. They have believed and been burned too many times.

I headed south now on Colorado 13 to Meeker, Rifle, and finally Grand Junction to visit my sister Jo. First I had to replace this depression with something more tuned to my walking, to my adventure.

When I was about ten miles south of Craig I saw some movement in the sagebrush at the side of the road. I stopped and watched. A few cars still raced down the road, but as I watched the sagebrush I realized there were over sixty antelopes amongst the bushes. They were leisurely eating their morning snack, ignoring the world. The people in the cars could see nothing but sagebrush. Walking on the road, I could see the magnificence of a wild and speedy animal. I spent almost a half an hour watching the herd. The antelope kept watching me and they slowly drifted away.

Later I saw several deer eating with the cattle in a field. I saw some coyotes going home from their night's hunting, and several jackrabbits and cottontails.

The animal that meant the most to me was a fox, a big red tailed fox. I was resting at the beginning of a large cut through a hill when I saw it first. It was racing toward the cut from the low hills to the west. It disappeared behind the hill, but soon reappeared at the crest of the cut, looking down at me. I stood up and put my pack on as the fox watched. As I walked south, the fox watched me, and then walked parallel to my path, but on the crest of the cut.

I stopped occasionally and watched the fox with my little telescope. The fox did not appear to be afraid of me, but instead I thought she appeared very curious. The road through the cut was about a quarter of a mile long. As I passed about the center of the cut, the fox disappeared down the other side. Soon the fox reappeared about a hundred yards further down the cut. The fox ran down the cut, crossed the road, and climbed the cut on the other side. From this vantage point she watched me as I walked along the road. The fox was much closer now and with my telescope I could see the characteristics of the fox's face. She was beautiful. Her eyes were sparkling and her hair actually glowed in the sunlight. The last thing I saw of her was when she grinned at me, winked, and then disappeared down the far side of the hill. When I walked out of the cut I looked back and tried to see her again, but I couldn't. She had melted into the hills.

The smile and the wink of that beautiful fox made me realize that this walking adventure I was on was not for my past. The adventure was for now, for the present, and for the future. My past determined what I was, but I could determine what I will be from now on, and I would not feel sorry for myself because I was alive and others were not. I would not be sad because buildings I thought should last forever did not. My world was ahead of me. Craig was behind me.

My pace quickened, my pack seemed lighter and most of my melancholy attitude was left behind. I was glad there were foxes in this world, and glad to be again on the road for this long walk home.

There were several sights during the day. I walked through Hamilton. As a boy, we used to turn east there to go fishing up the White River. It had grown beyond the single building I remembered. I passed the old Streeter Mine, that I remembered was always burning. I still saw some smoke, but I'm not sure if it was from the mine. I went through Axial and arrived in Meeker late.

Meeker was also a town that appeared to be dying. There were too many 'For Sale' signs for such a small town. Oil shale had been a big gainer for Meeker, but there was no requirement for oil shale when our national energy policy changed. Now there was only hunting and fishing to keep the city alive. I was very tired, but I still didn't sleep well. Craig still grasped at my mind too much. The motel where I slept was owned by the mayor and her husband. As we were talking on a beautiful summer evening she told me what I had heard so many times before, "This is the most wonderful place in all the world." I believed her.

The next day I headed out of Meeker to Rifle. The thing that bothered me more on this portion of the road was power lines. All across the country there were power lines. They often interfered with beautiful views; they always appeared grotesque on the side of a mountain. Along the valley heading into Rifle, a valley only a little over a quarter of a mile wide, there were three huge sets of power lines. The beauty of the valley was destroyed, completely, by these enormous aluminum and steel structures and the lines between the towers.

The garbage along the side of the road was bad, but the power lines were equally abhorrent. I knew the power lines were necessary for life in the city, for industry to produce, but they were ugly. I hope in the coming years industry finds a better way to move electricity, some way that does not interfere with the natural beauty of nature.

Walking south after my night in Rifle was interesting. As a child I had passed this way many times. Now there was a new interstate, but the old road was still there. I chose the old road.

There was very little traffic on the old road so I could walk without fear of speeding cars. I could see the big trucks, the motor homes and travel trailers on the interstate. I could see the speeding cars and noisy buses. On my road there were few cars, and no trucks, buses or travel trailers. On the other side of my old road was the railroad and twice that morning I saw loaded heavy trains heading up the valley toward Rifle.

On both sides were hills over a thousand feet above the valley floor. To the west they were called the Book Cliffs and they extend well into Utah. On the east they were not as steep and they appeared far greener. They were beautiful hills with a myriad of colors in the steep cliffs and sloping sides. The valley was cut by the Colorado River that wandered back and forth across the valley floor.

About ten-thirty an old station wagon passed me and stopped. The driver got out and came back to talk to me. I had not taken a break yet, so I was glad to stop and talk. The driver introduced himself as Hal, a rancher up on the side of the hill. He was tall with dark blond hair and he wore no hat. He had an engendering smile that made me like him immediately. He was an energetic man in his late thirties who was overwhelmed by my walking adventure. We talked for a while and he invited me to lunch. I explained that I did not want a ride and he understood. He pointed up the road and said he would like me to join him for lunch at the next exit. I asked him how far and he said it was about five miles. I told him I would be there in a little over an hour. We shook hands and he left.

As lunch time approached I came to the exit from the highway, but there were no restaurants. There were no buildings at all. The four-lane interstate was to my right and on the other side was the railroad. A small road from the little town of Rulison came under the railroad and was apparently the reason for the highway exit.

I did not see my host so I decided that when he said 'next exit' he meant the 'next exit,' not this exit. I was not worried for I had lunch in my pack and time on my hands so I headed on down the road. I walked only about a hundred yards when I heard a horn honk. I turned and there was the rancher in his station wagon under the train tracks in the shade. He had stopped his car in the right lane in the shade of the overpass.

I turned and walked back to his car. He had brought his wife and their three children. As I approached the car, he waved and took a card table from the station wagon. He placed it directly in front of the car that sat in the right lane of the road. He explained that there was practically no traffic. They had a tablecloth, chairs, and a complete lunch with sandwiches and fresh salad. They talked about how great it was living out in the country, away from the crime in the cities. They both explained that this was the greatest place in the world. I agreed.

When the two older children finished, they excused themselves and took garbage bags from the car and began picking up garbage along the sides of the road. The parents explained that it was important that when they left a place it should be significantly better than when they arrived. It was.

I recalled when Yvonne and I were Girl Scout leaders that this same lesson was what we tried to teach. It would be a nice lesson for the whole world to learn. Not just individuals, but organizations should learn this lesson. When you walk alone you become too idealistic. It was a good thought though.

I enjoyed the rest of my walk that day to Parachute, where I found a nice motel room and a great night's sleep. Parachute's claim to fame was apparently a golf course. I couldn't remember having heard of Parachute before. When I asked a local police officer, I found that it used to be Grand Valley, but they changed the name to Parachute. I liked the name Grand Valley better, but I'm sure they had a great reason to change the name.

As I was walking toward Grand Junction I passed Palisade. I attended my junior year of high school there, but very little was familiar to me. On the cliffs overlooking Palisade I could see the tailing from the old Garfield Mine. My brother-in-law owned the Garfield Mine and I worked there briefly back in 1946.

I was looking down on the peach trees near town when I remembered that I worked on one of those peach ranches. In Colorado peaches grow on ranches. Wheat grows on farms. This ranch was owned by a large family and I was their only employee. One evening we were walking back to the house and I was walking with the youngest son. He was about twenty-two and had been married for about three years. He commented that when he got home he was going to have a cold Coors, take his wife to bed and then relax with a cigarette. That seemed like a great evening to a sixteen year old. Later I was walking with his father. He mentioned that when he got home he was going to have a nice dry martini, a big rare porterhouse steak and then relax with a Havana cigar. I could understand where that would be an enjoyable evening. As we approached the house I walked with the 'old man.' He told me that when he got home he was going to have a shot of Jack Daniel's, take a good crap, and relax with a pipe. I guess I could understand that being enjoyable also.

I decided that life was enjoyable if you had a drink before and a smoke after, what went in-between depended upon your age. Now, walking across the United States I had given up smoking completely but my occasional red wine was sufficient to be a 'drink after.' I still enjoyed life, however.

On Tuesday I headed for Grand Junction and a visit with my sister, Jo, and her husband, Bill. I had met Bill previously, but only for a very short time. I do know that I felt uneasy about him, that I felt we were not friends. Jo had been my guardian through some of my rebellious teenage times. I had been back to see her on a few occasions, but I never felt comfortable with her. I always felt that I had not lived up to all she wanted me to be.

At the age of fifty-nine, just ten days short of sixty, I was sure I was mature enough that I could put most of those concerns behind me. I wanted to see Jo and reestablish family ties. I liked her children in Denver so much that I was sure I could.

Toward the middle of the afternoon I accepted a six mile ride around DeBeque Canyon. This allowed me to arrive in Grand Junction well before dark. At a service station I got direction to Jo's house. The directions were wrong. I have never had correct directions from service station attendants, yet I was dumb enough to ask them again. I found a mailman and he gave me the correct directions.

I arrived at Jo's house and spent the next couple of days there. I met her daughter, Pippie, again. Her name may be Susan to the rest of the world, but it was Pippie to me. Pippie was Jo's oldest and as a baby I had enjoyed Pippie. She came out to California with Paul back in 1959 and I had seen her again when we visited there some ten years later. Now she was a divorced single mother of two very enjoyable, if spoiled, young ladies, Jessica and Meridith. She was a responsible person in the community with a high position in the local welfare office.

I also spent several hours with Bill and we established a very satisfactory relationship. My time with Jo allowed us to reestablish some very firm family ties. On many of our previous visits either she or I were unhappy with life. This time we were both in a position where life was good and our relationship was great.

I visited the Kiwanis and was invited for an interview on the local television news. I often watched the evening news and always felt that it was well researched. They invited me to come to the station at five-fifteen. I did, with my pack. The receptionist asked me what I was there for and I told her. She nodded and left the room. A short time later another person came by and told me to go down to the studio. He pointed to the door and left. I went through the door and down to the studio. I arrived during a commercial. The newsman introduced himself and led me to the chair in front of the camera at his side. We had held no discussion before, so he had no idea of what I was doing other than that I was walking across the United States for Kiwanis.

When the commercial was over the newsman went directly into our interview. I felt very comfortable with it. The next day, at the Kiwanis noon meeting, only one person mentioned having seen the interview. I knew no one was watching, so I felt very relaxed.

I had another interview after the noon meeting with a different television station. It was short and, I felt, poorly edited. My next television time would come in another month as I approached Sonora Pass, but that was a long way ahead.

I waited an extra day with Jo and Bill in Grand Junction. I waited because my daughter, Karen, was due to have our second grandchild. She had a daughter, Michelle, on August second. My wife called to tell me all was well, the baby was healthy, and I should come on home. Talking to her reminded me how much I missed her.

My wife and daughters were very concerned about what lay ahead, walking across the Utah desert. At first I assured them there was no big problem, because I didn't really think there was a major problem. But my wife explained that our daughters were more than just concerned, they were deeply worried. They really believed that I could die crossing the desert. I tried to assure her that I would be all right. I think she believed me, but my daughters didn't.

Jo said she would help solve the problem. She talked to my wife for quite some time and convinced my wife that she would make sure that I was not in danger. She asked Yvonne to assure our daughters that their dad was in good hands. That seemed to satisfy everyone.

I decided to lower my pack weight so I could increase my walking speed. I went through my pack and shipped everything I could possibly do without. I shipped my long pants, keeping only one pair of shorts. I shipped my long sleeve shirt, keeping only two tee shirts. I shipped my sleeping bag and pad. I shipped all my mementos and any small items I had collected. My pack was reduced from thirty-five pounds to twenty-seven pounds. 'Light and fast' was what I wanted.

Utah

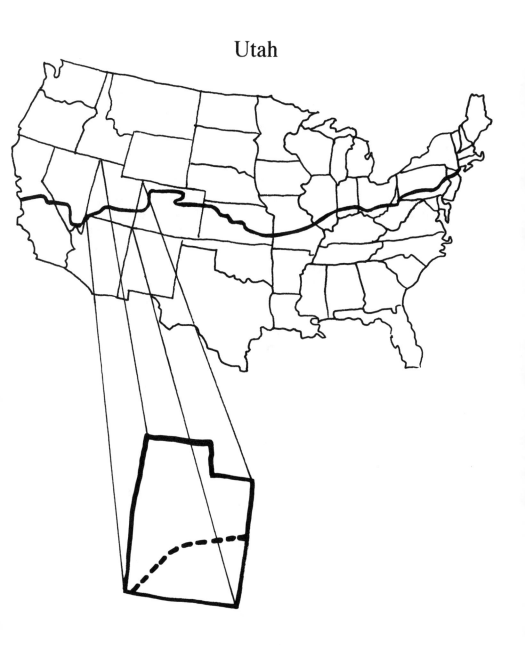

Utah

I was less than three weeks from Sonora, and I wanted to go home.

Jo did more than drive me part way across the Utah desert. She came out to see me each evening as I crossed the desert of Utah. She would often come out shortly after lunch and take me to the next town. She made certain that I would be comfortable crossing.

When we got to Salina I told Jo that she had done enough. I thanked her and we shared a big hug. She was a very dear friend and a great sister. I called my wife that evening and we had a long talk. I explained to her what Jo had done, but she said Jo had already told her. We talked about our daughters. They wanted me to come home and forget this silly adventure of mine. I told my wife I would soon be home. I'm sure the message was relayed to my daughters. There were no more big bad spots. She asked about Nevada but I lied, I told her it would be easy. I was missing home and Yvonne more every day. Yvonne assured me that all was well and that she missed me as well.

From Richfield on Sunday morning I walked south on US 89 that ran parallel to Interstate 15. There was little traffic, a cool comfortable day and I was headed for home. I felt good. I headed down to Sevier then south on US 89 to Big Rock Candy Mountain, Junction, Panguitch, and Mt. Carmel over the next four days.

At one point during a hot afternoon I discovered that I was out of water. It was still seven miles to Mt. Carmel so I knew I wouldn't die of thirst, but I was thirsty. I took out one of my empty flasks and as a car approached I held up the container. As the car passed I turned the container upside down. I felt that this would indicate that I was out of water. It was the first time I had ever asked for help in this manner and I wasn't sure how well it would work.

It worked very well. The first car that I asked for help stopped. The driver actually slammed on his breaks and skidded to a stop and backed up quickly to answer my call. He filled all three of my water containers, gave me two Cokes and a large lemon.

My cash was running a little low and I was concerned. Just before I had left Sonora I had received a VISA card in the mail. It had a limit of $3500. I estimated $3500 would be sufficient for the trip. However, I was spending more time in motels than I had planned and I was eating a great deal more than I had planned. I knew I was approaching the limit of my plastic as I approached Panguitch, Utah. I went into a local bank and asked for $350 to be charged on my card. I knew that would exceed the limit, but possibly I could find out by how much and then plan accordingly.

I was very surprised when they brought me the $350. I used my plastic for a few other motels after that and it was always accepted. After I got home I asked my wife about my exceeding the limit. She explained, "You kept charging and I kept paying so they raised your limit to seven thousand." I was delighted. My wife smiled knowingly at me and said, "Now give me the card." I did. I don't like plastic that much anyway.

*****

Cattle along the road would either move to get away from me, occasionally running, or they would move toward me and follow me along the side. I decided if man had fed them on a regular basis, they followed me and they expected me to feed them. This was also common with horses. If the cattle were more wild and depended on the grass in the fields for their food, then I was a possible enemy to be avoided and they would walk or run away from me.

A whole heard of fifty or sixty animals would watch me as I walked by. I was an unusual sight and something to be watched. The calves would watch for a while, but other things seemed more important, particularly other young animals. They didn't worry about me as long as the adults didn't worry. Occasionally one of the closer steers would run away and then most turned and ran away with them. Then the calves would run too.

At one point in Utah, I was walking along the road and several cattle were watching me. I had noticed that the fence was in need of repair, but didn't think any more about it.

A car coming toward me honked and I waved. Then a second one honked. I waved and as it passed I looked back. I was completely surprised. Behind me were six bovines in a line following me. I stopped and waved my arms at them but they did not move. I decided there was nothing I could do, so I continued walking.

I walked fast, so did the cattle. I walked slowly, so did the cattle. When I stopped, they stopped. At one point there were eleven, four-footed beasts following me. When I came to a bridge, the lead steer stopped. I continued across the bridge but they stayed on the other side.

It was about fifteen minutes until the road turned. When I looked back just before the curve, they were still standing there, looking at me as if expecting me to come back and feed them. I wondered how long they stood there.

*****

People often stopped their cars just to talk to me or to find out what I was doing. As I was walking toward Carmel a small car stopped and a very big man got out and we started talking. He asked, "What do you do?"

I replied, "I have a used book store in Sonora. Sonora, California."

He smiled broadly and said, "I have the opportunity of a lifetime for you." He went on to explain that he had exclusive rights to a particular species of house plant. He told me the Latin name, but I don't speak Latin . I don't remember what it was. The leaves of this plant could be used to make a tea that cured the common cold. He mentioned several other things it did too, but curing the common cold impressed me.

Since he had exclusive rights to this plant, he was willing to sell me exclusive rights to California for this plant. He went on about how rich I could get, how women became addicted to this plant and would do anything to get the leaves. He emphasized the word anything.

He wrote his name and address on a small piece of paper and gave it to me. I told him I would get back to him. He didn't really smile as he folded himself back into his little car and drove away. It has been my experience that in the real world the chance of a lifetime comes once about every six months.

From Carmel I headed west on Utah 9 to Zion National Park. In Zion there is a tunnel, and that presented me a major problem. The tunnel had no place to walk and I wasn't sure how long it was either. It was late afternoon so I decided I would walk through the tunnel. Just as I was about to enter the tunnel a ranger pulled up in his car. "You are not going to walk through that tunnel, are you."

I didn't know if it was question or a statement. The serious look on his face answered for me the question of my walking through the tunnel. Luckily I didn't have a smart answer so I just looked dumb.

"Get in. I'll give you a ride to Springdale." He was an exceptionally nice person. He had several homilies for me. 'Live and let live.'—'If you can help, we need you. If you can't help, please don't interfere.'—'Keep away from people who don't smile back.'—'Two good friends are the most a person can handle. Few have two good friends, some have one, most don't have any.' I'm certain he gave me others.

I spent the night camped next to a river in Zion National Park and early the next morning started walking toward home. Next stop, St. George, Utah.

I had expected that by this time in the trip, I would be in great shape, able to walk all day and not feel tired. It was just the opposite. My feet and legs hurt in many of the joints and the pain was considerable. Tylenol was my constant companion. The pain was similar to what I felt when I was first started, except now I was far more tired. I decided that I had pushed my sixty year old body to the extreme. My only consolation was that it was less than a month until the walk would be over, less than three weeks until I would be home in Sonora for a day of rest.

Just past Zion I went through Virgin, Utah. I asked a construction worker to take my picture under the welcome sign. I missed having my picture taken in Pennsylvania when I went by the road to Intercourse. I loved the city names.

As I approached St. George I had to walk on Interstate 15. In talking to various law enforcement people I decided it was all right to walk on an interstate if there was no other route available. Near the end of the walk to St. George there was an alternate route, but it was longer, so I decided to stay on the interstate.

As I came up over the crest of a hill I saw a highway patrolman about a quarter mile ahead giving a ticket to a truck driver. The patrolman also saw me.

He smiled at me as only a highway patrol officer can smile, absolute power. I knew I'd had it. I considered going back to the on-ramp, but that was about a mile back, and I do not like backtracking. I continued on the interstate. When I came to the truck and the patrol car, I walked several feet on the inside and the patrolman didn't see me.

I had walked about five minutes past the vehicles when I heard a yell. It was the patrolman yelling at me. I think he was motioning for me to come back. As I said, I do not like to backtrack, so I pretended I didn't understand him. If he was going to give me a ticket, he was going to have to come to me, I wasn't going to him. This little charade went on for three or four minutes. He appeared to be getting angry.

As he approached his car to come back to me, a small red sports car buzzed by us going at least ninety miles per hour. The patrolman looked at me and yelled something while shaking his fist in the air, then jumped in his car and sped after the little red sports car. I immediately headed out for the next exit, thankful for little red sports cars.

In St. George I was welcomed by the St. George Kiwanis President and the press. They had arranged a very comfortable room at the Comfort Suites with a Jacuzzi. I took full advantage of it. I also discovered that southern Utah was called Dixie. I was told that there were many southerners in the area and it was named for their support for the southern cause, besides, it was in 'Southern' Utah. There was a big thirty foot 'D' on the side of the hill above St. George for Dixie State College.

Nevada

Nevada

From St. George I took the bus to Las Vegas. This didn't really fit with my 'walking.' I was a bit behind schedule. I had to be in San Francisco on September 7. I did enjoy the ride. In Las Vegas the Kiwanis Club arranged a reduced rate at a strip hotel for me. I walked from the bus station that was downtown to the MGM Marina on the strip.

I had forgotten about Las Vegas and the contradictions that were everywhere. The wedding chapel was between a gambling casino and an all night mini mart. There was a $60,000 Mercedes following a 1938 beat-up Chevrolet into the valet parking. I saw a tall, attractive show girl pushing a baby carriage into a liquor store. It was a cool summer evening as I walked the seven miles to the MGM Marina.

The room was reasonably priced, with the discount, and I slept well. I slept well until about seven o'clock in the morning when the fire alarm screamed into my room. I recalled the fire that the MGM Grand had experienced several years back, so my adrenaline flowed. I dressed, remembering my problem in Kansas, and checked to see if the door was hot. It wasn't so I opened it and checked the hallway. I could smell no smoke. I did see other guests looking down the hall with the same concern I had. I tried to call the desk, but they never answered; they were too busy with other calls. About ten minutes after the initial alarm a voice came from a box on the wall and asked everyone to excuse the alarm. They said they were checking as to the cause, but they assured us that nothing was wrong. Finally the voice came back and announced that it was a false alarm and they hoped it hadn't bothered us. They said that they had the state of the art equipment to protect everyone. I believed every word they said, so I packed up and moved out. I couldn't go back to sleep after being awakened by a fire alarm.

I had been very concerned about the heat of Nevada. I had lived in Las Vegas for almost five years, and I knew how hot it could get, but the next few days were cool and very comfortable. The first couple days I walked on a four lane highway built to handle the traffic to and from the Nevada Test Site. Immediately after passing the Mercury turnoff late on my second full day out of Las Vegas, US 95 decreased from four large lanes with large shoulders to two narrow lanes with little or no shoulders.

Lathrop Wells was comfortable and so was Beatty. I planned on walking to Scotty's Junction. The waitress in Beatty said she thought there was a motel in Scotty's Junction. In the late afternoon, as I approached Scotty's Junction, I peered ahead with my little telescope and I saw an 'Open' sign. When I saw the 'Open' sign, I knew I was going to have a great night's rest.

The 'Open' was not in front of a motel however nor was it in front of a gas station. It was in front of a bordello. I was surprised, but I was also concerned. After Las Vegas I had spent a night in a culvert, and I didn't want another night like that, but it looked as if I had no choice. I could not afford a bed for the night in a bordello.

As I was standing in front of the bordello, wondering what I should do, I watched as a big black Chrysler passed heading north. It went about a mile up the road and turned around and returned. It pulled into the parking lot. A large, well built, bearded man stepped out and walked over to me. He said, "You're Matt Mattingly, aren't you."

I nodded, not knowing who he was or how he knew my name. He continued, "I'm Tom Katosic from Big Oak Flat." Big Oak Flat was a small town about fifteen miles from Sonora. "I'm one of your customers at the bookstore." I was elated. We talked for a few minutes. Tom and his wife, Candace, were coming back from a convention in Las Vegas. They had discussed the possibility of seeing me and were excited that they had. He asked if there was anything he could do for me.

I said there was. I asked, "Could you drive me to Goldfield?" He said they could and they did. They offered to take me all the way to Sonora, but I declined. I had come too far to accept a ride over pleasant country. I appreciated the offer though. I was glad I had a bookstore and I was glad my weekly reports in Sonora had been read. I was glad for Tom because I didn't want another night out without my sleeping bag. I also didn't want a night in a bordello either. That would be hard to explain to my wife when the credit card was grossly overrun.

In Goldfield I stayed at the Sundog Bed and Breakfast. The waitress in Beatty had recommended it. The owners were an Irish lass, Maire, and her Canadian husband, David. They worked at the Tonapah Test Range, ran the bed and breakfast and Maire was running for county commissioner. They were great people and they had a fine bed and breakfast. The next morning Maire fixed me an exceptional breakfast of bacon, eggs, fresh bread and lots of potatoes.

The next day I walked to Tonapah. I did accept a three mile ride from Maire, because I told her the night before that I would. Besides, I knew she had a big delicious roast beef sandwich with extra onions in the front seat of the car waiting for me.

I had an interview in Tonapah and the next day I headed west on US 6, and with a couple small rides totaling about six miles, I made it to

Basalt. Tomorrow I would enter California. The trip was almost over. I slept well that night with thoughts of home, with thoughts of Yvonne, with thoughts of our bookstore.

California

California

I intended to only go twenty miles the next day to Benton and then west on US 120 to Lee Vining. When I arrived in Benton I found there was no motel. It was here that my planning had not sufficed. I had passed a motel where US 6 crossed the state line, but I had decided to go further. I should have taken it slower and stayed at the state line motel, but it was too late now. I proceeded on down to Bishop, with the help of a short ride in the back of a bouncing Jeep.

In Bishop I made two purchases. I bought a pair of long pants and a long sleeve shirt. It was getting cool again. The next day I would be going over seven thousand feet and it was late August. The mornings and nights were very cool. I needed more clothes.

From Bishop I headed north on US 395, up a long grade and spent the night at a Youth Hostel at the top. It was very pleasant, comfortable and the company there was great. I had a delicious breakfast, cooked with loving care by the proprietor of the hostel. I proceeded north to spend the night a few miles past Mammoth Lakes.

The walk that day was typical, sometimes great and other times almost disastrous. I walked on the new four lane road. The cars had two lanes and I had two lanes. The road was just about finished, but it wasn't open to auto traffic yet, only foot traffic. It made a pleasant day walking through the pine trees on a broad road. But it also rained a lot and I got very wet. The rain storms were never announced, they just came down and I didn't have time to find shelter or cover my pack or my self, so I got wet. I had to change socks five times because they were too wet. It hailed once, and I had to flip my cover over the top to protect me from the stones. My shoes became soaked so I changed them.

When I reached the turn-off to June Lake I had to make another decision. It was two miles off my path to June Lake or eleven miles ahead to Lee Vining. Both had motels. Though I had walked only about thirty miles, I was tired. My endurance was at its limit.

I recalled June Lake as being very pleasant from previous trips, so I took the two mile walk. Besides, I would get to rest sooner. The motel in June Lake was expensive. Tourist season in a recreational town usually was. I took my Tylenol and slept for about six hours. I was anxious to continue my walk.

Early Sunday morning I left June Lake, walked the two miles back to US 395 and then continued north. As I passed the second entrance into the June Lake loop, I heard a horn honking and I turned to give a thumbs up. The car pulled from the loop and stopped in front of me. I immediately recognized the woman who got out. She was Jackie from Sonora, another of my customers at the book store. She and her husband were on their way back to Sonora from their vacation in Arizona. We talked for some time and they drove me up US 395 about six miles.

They assured me they would relay to my wife that I was well. They offered to take me all the way to Sonora but I declined. As they waved and drove away I felt very good. With their lift, I would arrive in Bridgeport about four and get a good night's sleep.

Knowing I was ahead of schedule, I walked more slowly and dawdled a lot. I soaked my feet in a cool stream and relaxed. I was nearing the end of my walk, and I wanted to enjoy my accomplishment.

I arrived in Bridgeport late Sunday night. I had dallied too long. As I was eating supper a couple I knew very well from Sonora came into the restaurant, Koney and Pete. They were in a Kiwanis Club in Sonora. I hugged her and was very happy to see her. We talked for a long time about what had happened in Sonora during my three-and-a-half months' absence. The next morning we had breakfast together to continue our talk. I hadn't realized how homesick I was. My wife had arranged for me to meet a television crew on Monday morning in Bridgeport. At eight-thirty I met Miles Saunders and Kit Tyler from KCRA, the NBC television station in Sacramento.

Television interviews in Grand Junction had been great, but Miles and Kit wanted to do something more. They explained that what they wanted to do was encapsulate my trip in three minutes, allow viewers to feel my trip by watching 180 seconds of video. I knew that was impossible. I had too many experiences, too many adventures for television to capture more than just a hint in three minutes.

After talking with Miles and Kit, I agreed to try. They had an enthusiasm that I easily accepted. We drove sixty miles out to the desert and they asked me to walk across the sage brush and cactus landscape while they photographed my walk. I agreed for I had no trouble with walking, I would have been walking today anyway. I walked over three hundred yards into the desert and waited for their signal. They waved for me to come toward them. I did. They were not completely satisfied with my first attempt so I did it again, but more slowly.

Later we sat in the desert and talked about my trip with the cameras rolling the entire time. I walked along the roads and across the roads. At times the television camera was pointed toward me, other times it was filming the desert or occasionally, Miles. Miles and Kit made me feel very comfortable and completely at ease. Finally they drove back to Bridgeport, where we had lunch, and then headed north on US 395 to the cutoff to Sonora Pass.

We drove part way up US 108, the road across Sonora Pass. The sign as we left US 395 said, "CAUTION 27% Grade." If there was that steep of a grade, it was only for a very short distance. We stopped twice and I walked up the pass for a short distance while their cameras were rolling.

They drove me to the top of Sonora Pass and they took several minutes of pictures. I yelled for them as I walked across the top of the pass. They were surprised at the volume of my yell. I was loud. They asked me to repeat my yell for their cameras again. I did.

I think what surprised them the most was the way I was treated by some casual motorists who had stopped at the top of the pass. Miles and I were talking at the top of the pass and two cars stopped and some people came over to me. They recognized me and exclaimed their happiness at seeing me.

Miles and Kit recorded the scene. We talked after the visitors left and I asked if there was any additional footage they needed. They said they thought they had what they needed. They offered to drive me back down to Bridgeport. I declined. They offered to drive me back to US 395. I declined. Then they offered to drive me a couple miles back down the pass so I could walk back up. I declined. I hate to backtrack. Besides, the day had been very enjoyable.

They left me at the top of Sonora Pass. I knew that soon my wife would be arriving. Another major goal of my walk had been completed. I was at the top of the Sierra Nevada, the top of Sonora Pass. I sat by the side of the road.

*****

This walk was reaching the end, but I wondered if there would be others. I wanted to return to my home and my bookstore. There were enough chores around the house to keep me busy for at least five years, but what then? I knew that I would do something else. I hoped it wouldn't be quite this elaborate, and I knew it would not be this long. Four months away from home just to satisfy a quest would no longer be acceptable. One month would be acceptable, anything over two months would not be acceptable.

I missed the regularity of everyday living. I had imposed a certain false regularity on my trip. The regularity that every morning I had to get up and walk. I was tired of that. I wanted a change in my lifestyle, my false life style, to something approaching what I had always believed was normal.

When I got up in the morning, I wanted to know where I was going to spend the night, with whom, in what bed, and where. I wanted some idea of what tomorrow held as far as surroundings, where would I be for lunch, and who would be there.

I knew when I got back to Sonora that for the first few days my trip would be all-important. After that, attention for my travels would subside. I expected that. I knew that when I first finished my walk I would be a local celebrity. But I also knew that in three months, the walk would have been forgotten by most, but not all, and never by me.

After the pair of television interviewers left on Monday afternoon, I sat at the top of Sonora Pass thinking about my trip. I had come a little less than three thousand five hundred miles, spent three and a half months, met hundreds of people and I was tired. I leaned my pack against a tree and sat down next to it to watch the cars and trucks cross the pass.

I wasn't sure who would be coming up to meet me other than Yvonne. I knew she would be here. After today I had two days to walk to Sonora. On Thursday morning I would attend the Kiwanis meeting. I had asked Bud Vogel, a Kiwanian at The Union Democrat, to make sure I was the guest speaker. He said he would.

As I rested I saw a man walked over the crest of the hill from a parking lot on the other side. It was Arnie, one of my brother Kiwanians from Sonora. We shook hands, hugged and he said he had planned on driving down the other side of Sonora Pass to meet me. I didn't tell him I had a ride up.

Soon other cars came up. Two were filled with Kiwanians and one carried a reporter from The Union Democrat, Chris Bateman. Chris conducted an excellent interview, but then he had walked, hiked and traveled a great deal, so he knew a lot of my thinking, and the pertinent questions. His write-up and his pictures about my trip were among the best. Chris took lots of pictures and asked a lot of questions. My fellow Kiwanians were happy to see me. I knew, because they gave me a hard time.

One of the Kiwanians was Leetta Nutting. During the trip she had written me a letter and sent me money to assist me on my trip. She said she would have joined me for the entire trip if I would have asked her. I thought I had asked every attractive woman.

We stood around and talked about the changes in Sonora since I had been gone. There were not many. The new Taco Bell had been completed, including a new traffic light. Some work had been done on the Sullivan Creek Bridge but it wasn't completed yet. Dick Nutting, Leetta's husband, was in the run-off election for Sheriff. George Segarini had lost his attempt to become a County Supervisor. That was about all. In general, everything was as I had assumed it to be.

We talked a while longer as the sun was beginning to set. Leetta asked me if Yvonne was coming. She was worried since she was not yet here. I assured her that nothing had happened to Yvonne, and that she would be there as soon as she was able to come.

I knew Yvonne was running late because she would have to stop by our home to pick up her dog, Lacey. Lacey was her dog, a wire-haired terrier that hated me. It was almost mutual. I dislike dogs that will not 'come' when I command 'come.' Lacey would not 'come'. In fact, Lacey would not do anything I told her to do. Lacey was the first dog we ever had that would not respond to me. Perhaps that's why I had so many problems with her. Yvonne suggested that it was difficult to train a dog when the dog was smarter than the master.

Finally I looked down the road and saw Yvonne's white Thunderbird coming up. I left the group and walked over to a place that I had reserved for her to park. She pulled into the parking place, smiled, and quickly stopped. She jumped from the car and we kissed, hugged and kissed some more. It had been three-and-a-half months since I had held her in my arms. I held her a long time and told her how much I loved her. I was glad to be in her arms again. It had been a very long walk home. Lacey did not even recognize my presence. So much for her.

Chris took some more pictures and finally I got in the car with Yvonne. She drove because I didn't have my license and I hadn't driven a car for nearly four months. It was arranged that Birge, another Kiwanian, would pick me up the next morning at our home and drive me back up to the top of Sonora Pass. I fully expected, and wanted, some of the members of the Kiwanis Club to join me in the walk down the hill, but they all chickened out. They didn't want to be out-walked by an old man. The reason I wanted some company was that I could slow down some. Since none did, I would keep to my four miles per hour pace.

Monday night I slept at home in our water bed. I knew that I would be sleeping there for the next three nights. That was unique, to know where I was going to sleep the next night. It was good to be home.

On Tuesday morning Birge picked me up and took me to the top of the pass. I started my walk shortly after eight, and I was now walking in my home county of Tuolumne. That was good. I also started with a brand new pair of Rockports. The road was downhill and I felt perfect. It took almost a half an hour before the perfection ended and my first blister popped. I took off my new shoes and returned to the worn pair.

The day was comfortable and I headed downhill to Strawberry. I tried to get some lunch at Dardanelles, but the cafe was closed. I bought two Twinkies, a Pepsi and a couple of apples and headed on down.

Shortly after six Tuesday evening Yvonne picked me up, one half mile from Strawberry. She brought her sister, Dorothy, with her. Dorothy had been running the bookstore during most of the summer, so we talked a lot about business. Dorothy made it possible for me to take this walk. She handled the bookstore Tuesday through Friday. Yvonne was there on Saturdays. Yvonne had also taken the store for a week and my daughter, Doreen, had taken it for a week. Dorothy had to spend some time with her husband. I might have lost a brother-in-law out of this walk, but I doubted it. He probably enjoyed the time alone.

Wednesday morning Yvonne drove me up the road just short of Strawberry and left me off. Today was going to be my big day, my day in the sun at Sonora. Tuesday's Sonora Union Democrat had three front page pictures of my crossing the summit and there was a very long article about it. They invited everyone to Coffill Park on Wednesday at four in the afternoon to see me. The Kiwanis Club planned to be there and several others would be there. I knew Yvonne would be there. Dorothy said she was closing the store and coming down. Also my daughter, Karen, and my grandson, Kevin, would be there. Karen was bringing Michelle, my granddaughter who was only a month old, my granddaughter whom I had never seen. I was nervous, nervous about all the attention, nervous about all the people that would be there, nervous about what I would say.

Another change from previous days on my trip was the number of horns honking at me. Several people had read the newspaper articles and when they saw my pack, they honked and yelled. Several stopped to congratulate me. I shook hands with the men, but I hugged the women and the children.

Shortly after lunch a car stopped me and the driver said a local radio station, KKBN in Twain Harte, wanted to have me stop by the station for an interview. It seemed like a good idea to me. The driver took me to the station and I had an excellent interview with a newly hired announcer, Tim. When I was through, I walked back to the highway and I had to re-walk a couple miles.

Shortly after getting back on the road another car stopped. It was a rather dilapidated rusty car. The driver introduced himself as Russell Frank, a reporter from the Modesto Bee. We sat at the side of the road and I again had one of my better interviews. Russell also took some pictures and his article was well done. He was a good reporter.

The closer to Sonora I got, the more often the horns honked. The big logging trucks often blasted their loud air horns to me. I would return with a strong 'thumbs up.' I was now giving a 'thumbs up' to all approaching traffic. My emotions were running very high. My pace quickened and I had a broad smile on my face. It was a perfect day.

As I passed Standard Road, about five miles east of Sonora, Leetta Nutting joined me. She walked with me the rest of the way to Sonora. I had invited several people along the 3000 miles to walk with me, but this was the first time on the entire trip that anyone had actually joined me. Leetta had more guts than most; my kind of woman.

About a half mile later we passed a branch of the El Capitan Bank. My wife worked for El Capitan, but not at this branch. It didn't matter. As I approached everyone from the bank came out and clapped and yelled. Leetta and I went over and I received hugs from all the women. I checked the time and decided that I was ahead of schedule, so when they offered me a cup of coffee I accepted. Leetta didn't drink coffee.

As we passed Rube's Family Restaurant we stopped. This is where our Kiwanis Club meets and everyone knew who I was. That was a good feeling. I washed up and combed my hair and put on a clean tee shirt. I wanted to look good for the press and the crowd that I expected.

About two miles before town there was a narrow bridge, the Sullivan Creek Bridge. When getting in shape for my walk I had crossed this bridge many times, and I knew it was narrow. There was no room for a pedestrian. During the four months of my walk they had worked on the bridge. They were going to widen it to five lanes. The two lanes I had crossed many times was gone. Now there were two lanes of new bridge, but there was still no room for pedestrians.

I did not want my long walk to end with an accident this close to home so Leetta and I went under the bridge and came up on the other side. In this diversion I slipped and got dirt and dust on my hands, face and pack. So much for trying to look good for the reception.

A few blocks before Coffill Park, where my reception was to be, we passed the bank where Yvonne worked. She joined us for the last bit. I was emotionally very high. Chris Bateman from the paper took several pictures during the last block.

I arrived at Coffill Park at 3:30, thirty minutes ahead of schedule, but I didn't care. Several people were there and lots more were coming. They had a ceremony planned for me at four so I had time to relax and talk to my friends before the formalities began. I tried to calm down, but I couldn't.

Just as the introductions were being made, Karen arrived with Kevin and Michelle. Kevin and I had always been close. Every time Yvonne talked with him while I was gone, he wanted to know where I was and when would I be home. Yvonne bought him a jigsaw puzzle of the United States and every time they worked it Yvonne would show him where I was. I missed Kevin and he apparently had missed me.

As Kevin came down to the park, I was in front of a crowd of about fifty. One of our verbose Kiwanians, Harlan Dunning, was giving me an enormous buildup. Kevin saw me and he ran through all the crowd, raced across the open space and into my open arms. He hugged me and I hugged him. He hugged me for the next fifteen minutes, through the entire ceremony. I kept whispering to him that I had missed him and that I loved him. He always responded by hugging me tighter.

In the ceremony I was congratulated by the Tuolumne County Supervisors, by the Mayor of the City of Sonora and by the Director of the Chamber of Commerce. Each gave me a document with 'Whereas" and "Wherefore" written on them. I was proud of what I had done and I happily accepted them. With Kevin still in my arms, I thanked everyone and told them how happy I was to be back. I talked for about ten minutes. I hadn't planned any particular words, but just some general thoughts.

Occasionally, as I was talking, Kevin released his tight hold on me to turn around and check all the activity. Satisfied that all was well, he again hugged me. He often whispered that he loved me.

My welcome to Sonora was all that I could have wanted. My family and friends were there. My accomplishment was recognized. Soon I would be home and spend every night on our water bed. I was happy.

I attended the Kiwanis meeting the next morning. Bud had not arranged for me to be the speaker, but I got about fifteen minutes to tell them a few of the highlights of my trip. It was good to be back with the 'loudest and proudest' Kiwanis Club.

I went down to my bookstore for a while that afternoon and it felt great to walk among the books. I had left the bookstore clean and in good shape. It was now cleaner and in better shape than when I had left. I was glad Dorothy, my sister-in-law, had been there.

Early Friday morning I rode down to Sonora with Yvonne and Dorothy and continued my walk. Dick Nutting, Leetta's husband, joined me immediately and walked the three miles to Jamestown with me.

I did not like leaving Sonora. Even though I knew that in another week I would be back, I did not enjoy leaving home. I wanted to end this walk and get back to my bookstore. I was homesick again. I wanted to finish this walk.

I made it to Don Pedro Friday evening to spend a night with my brother-in-law, Ray, Dorothy's husband. I spent the next day there also, resting with my feet in the water and a glass of red wine in my hands.

On Sunday I went to Modesto and spent the night with Dorothy and Ray. On Monday, Labor Day, I went past Paterson and several miles up Del Puerto Canyon.

During the four months of my walk there were 153,567 cars that passed me three to ten feet away. The wind gusts, or wind-wake, generated by these vehicles varied by the age of the car, the speed of the car and the distance away. Generally the newer cars were more aerodynamic and had significantly less wind-wake.

Some trucks had huge wind-wakes while others had almost none. The worst wind-wake from trucks came from those that had unusual loads such as trucks carrying pipes or road repair equipment. Telephone company trucks and power company trucks were also notorious for their wind-wake. The rough contours and the uneven edges were the causes of these wakes.

*****

Of the 153,567 cars I met, most were traveling about sixty miles per hour so I would see the drivers only briefly, but I established a definite relationship with the drivers.

The drivers I classified into good drivers, bad drivers, little ol' lady drivers, he-man-macho drivers, salesmen drivers and the rest of them.

The best drivers on the road were, without question, the school bus drivers. They were attentive to the road, alert to everything ahead and they always had their hands on the steering wheel. The women bus drivers always returned my wave. The male bus drivers seldom did. I knew a male school bus driver in California named Jack. It was important to Jack that he appear mean to the kids so he could keep their respect. He was really a big teddy bear and the kids all knew that, but Jack didn't.

The worst drivers were not as easy to define. They drove older cars with a few dents and their license plates were usually at an angle.

Neither the driver nor anyone else wore seat belts and there were at least two, sometimes six, people in the car.

It didn't matter whether the driver was male or female, young or old, they were more concerned about the activities inside the car than they were about either the speed or the direction of the car. I noticed immediately that the drivers only had one hand on the wheel. The drivers often had an arm around either a child or a mate near by, a beer or soft drink in the other hand with a cigarette hanging from the lip. The driver was very concerned about who was doing what and where inside the car. These drivers were dangerous on the roads, not just to walkers, but to other drivers as well.

The little ol' lady drivers may also have been either young or old and either male or female, but they were easily identified. They drove a late model medium-sized vehicle painted a bland color. Their seat belts were always fastened, the drivers always had their hands properly positioned at ten and two with their eyes looking directly ahead. The drivers knew that they were entitled to the lane between the center line and the white line at the side. They would not veer one inch to avoid a poor walker, nor would they even turn their head to indicate that they recognized my existence. I decided that some of them may have turned their eyes, but only very quickly. The little ol' lady drivers were dangerous to a walker on the roads.

The ultimate he-man-macho driver vehicle had four-wheel drive, a roll bar with six KC lights on top, two large dogs in the back, large noisy tires and an engine without any noise abatement.

The he-man-macho driver had reflective sun glasses, with trendy colored cords attached, and he never returned my wave. At most he would raise a finger from the wheel, but usually he only wrinkled his upper lip to indicate his dislike for anyone so poor as to have to walk.

Salesman drivers were individuals who had traveled the same road many times. They usually had their right arm extended across the seat top, their heads were bobbing to the tune on the radio and their thoughts were on their next client or their last client or the girl last night, or something other than the road.

As the salesmen approached their cars often slipped slowly onto my shoulder area, and I would move further to the left. They would recognize what was happening before they got to me and they would turn back with a bewildered look on their face. I always watched for salesman drivers and stepped to the left to avoid any appearance of playing the game of chicken.

The majority of drivers were 'the rest of them': good drivers that moved toward the center to allow me the shoulder area. These drivers usually waved back and occasionally beeped their horns in recognition, but all drivers, even the good ones, had a bewildered and questioning look as they passed by.

One interesting thing about the cars were the number of them that had shaded windows, that is, windows darkened so it was impossible to see who was inside. I saw one car that even had them reflective so that not only was it impossible to see in, but you saw yourself. I have noticed that many people wear reflective dark glasses. Perhaps it is a sign that we don't want people to see what we're thinking.

On this long walk home I learned that if you took all the cars I have seen, lined them up end to end on an interstate, some he-man-macho driver with an out-of-state license in his ultimate vehicle would pass them all.

*****

I slept that night between two 'No Trespassing' signs. I could not find any place else to sleep and besides, the signs were old and they didn't say 'Really.'

The next morning I made it to the top of Mount Hamilton. From now on it was all downhill to San Francisco. On a clear day, it was possible to see San Francisco from Mount Hamilton. This was not a clear day. As I walked past the observatory a van stopped and an attractive young woman stepped out and introduced herself as Susie originally from Sonora but from Mount Hamilton now. She gave me a big hug. She explained that she had seen my picture in the Sonora paper and the previous day I had talked with her father-in-law coming up Mount Hamilton.

Susie was a very talkative person. She introduced me to most of the people 'on the hill.' They have a very tight, closely knit community there. I had lunch with the director of the Observatory and his wife. I enjoyed it tremendously. They had traveled extensively and were enjoyable to meet.

After lunch, Susie suggested that tomorrow I could visit their class. She explained that at Mount Hamilton there was a one room school house. The school included seven grades, kindergarten through sixth, with one teacher and one principal in one room. I accepted immediately. I enjoy talking to children. It was arranged that I would continue my walk down to Grant Park, ten miles, and Susie would pick me up the next morning at nine and bring me back to the class. Afterward, Susie would take me down the hill, past Grant Park and, depending upon the time, far enough to make up for the time visiting the class.

I headed down the hill and camped Tuesday night in Grant Park. I was alone in the park and found that very enjoyable. I had my bag in an open field where I could see all the world around me. I watched a couple of owls in the oak trees as they called back and forth. They decided it was dinner time and they silently glided from their perch to the ground below to eat. For the next couple hours they had several ground squirrels and chipmunks for dinner. Nature was seldom gentle to the weak, the small or the careless.

I was tired and I fell asleep earlier than I wanted to. I awoke the next morning, found a shower and when Susie arrived, I was eager to go.

I talked to the students at Mount Hamilton. I enjoyed it a great deal. Talking to children was far more enjoyable than talking to adults. The enthusiasm of children was real. The look of admiration in their eyes was honest. Their questions were the same ones adults asked, except the answers were important to them. I was particularly honored since it was their first day of school.

I talked with them far longer that I had planned and far longer than the teacher had planned also, I am sure. Susie then took me back down the hill and dropped me at the bottom, in San Jose.

One of the many times on my trip I used my compass was in San Jose. I had lived there for ten years. I had traveled all over the San Jose area when I lived there, but I was lost. I had no idea where I was. There were old freeways, new freeways and land cleared for additional freeways. None of these were here when I was here. The names of the streets were totally different from what I remembered. I was lost.

I was going to call the local Kiwanis Club, but I knew better than to call them. What would I answer when they asked, "Where are you?" I couldn't reply, "I don't know." I walked west on any street that would go that direction. If I couldn't go west, I went north. Two and a half hours later I finally found a place where I knew where I was. I had now walked completely through San Jose and was in Santa Clara. I was glad I had a compass.

Since I knew where I was I called the local Kiwanis Club and within minutes I was picked up by Steve, an enthusiastic Kiwanian. He took me to Sam, the local Lieutenant Governor. They arranged for interviews with the Santa Clara paper immediately and arranged for the San Jose Mercury-News to interview me the next day. Sam knew who to contact and what to say.

I didn't sleep a lot that night, but I did sleep well. The next morning I visited a Kiwanis Club in Los Gatos with Sam. And Sam arranged for the San Jose paper to take some pictures. With the pictures out of the way, Sam set me loose on El Camino Real, heading north. Sam had arranged for me to visit the noon Club in Palo Alto.

My speed must have been right because I arrived at the meeting one minute before it started. This was a very loud and raucous group, the kind I enjoyed the most.

The president, Neil, and his wife, both Kiwanians, invited me to spend my last night on the road with them. I agreed. It was arranged that I would continue walking up El Camino Real as far as I could. When I walked as far as I wanted, I would call Neil and he would come and pick me up. The next morning, Friday, he would take me back up El Camino Real and let me finish my walk.

That evening Neil and I had a scotch before dinner and it tasted great. Neil barbecued our steaks and we had a very relaxing evening. I retired early, but slept very little. My thoughts were moving too fast. I didn't know what to expect on my final day.

I knew Yvonne would meet me at the prearranged location, where the Great Highway meets Sloat Boulevard in San Francisco. I wasn't sure who else would be there. I had been given a number to call for police escort. I had been told that all the television networks would be there and that all the local new papers would be there. I was also told that the Kiwanis Governor, Bob Wiekoff, would be there as well a large contingent of Kiwanians from San Francisco and Sonora.

What sleep I did get, was not restful. Early the next morning Neil took me back up the peninsula and sent me on my way...the last day, and a fine day it was. The sky was clear, the temperature was perfect and the road was good. I called all the people I was supposed to call. No one was there when I called. My Kiwanis contact, Bill Talmadge, was out of the office, so I left a message. The man I had been told to call for the police escort was apparently not the person I was supposed to call. The television and newspapers were aware of me and planned to be there. So I walked north into San Francisco, apprehensive but high on the emotional ladder.

About eleven o'clock Bill Talmadge found me walking up the road and explained what was taking place. I was to meet him and some others for lunch about two miles further up the road and arrangements had been made for the meeting at the Great Highway and Sloat. He had called the press and he had sent them all press releases about my walk, and they assured him that they would be there. I was impressed with the confidence and knowledge of Bill Talmadge. I knew I was in good hands.

At lunch, only Talmadge was there, the others couldn't make it. I ate, but I was too nervous to really enjoy it. After lunch, Bill showed me where to head and what to expect. I took off and tried to keep calm. The walking helped, but I was getting excited. About half a mile before the meeting place, Bill again met me and explained exactly where I was to go. He said there was one camera man there and he said my wife was there. Things were beginning to feel great.

Conclusion

Conclusion

It was now time to conclude my odyssey. I had agreed to be at the meeting place at two o'clock. I had to walk very fast for the last few miles, since lunch, to make it, but at exactly two o'clock, I was at the Great Highway and Sloat as required. I could hear the waves on the beach, feel the salt breeze on my face and I saw Yvonne.

The cameraman that Bill had said was there was still there, but no others were. There was one Kiwanian there. I was never clear whether he just happened to be there or whether he had planned to be there, but there was one Kiwanian there.

I was expecting more than Yvonne, one television cameraman and one Kiwanian, but I couldn't change what was real. Yvonne joined me from our meeting place as we walked to the Golden Gate Bridge. It was slightly over eight miles and we left shortly after two. I planned to be at the Golden Gate Bridge by four.

The two hour walk was more than just a conclusion of a trip to me. I had first arrived in San Francisco in June 1950 as a Seaman Second Class in the United States Navy. I learned electronics on Treasure Island and lived there for nine months and I knew the city well. When I got out of the Navy in November 1953, I had opened a television repair shop in the Sunset district of San Francisco, just east of where we were now walking. I knew this part of San Francisco well. I had spent many hours on the beaches near where we were walking. This walk was a hike down memory lane for me, a trip through my past.

The area had not changed very much from what I remembered from 1953-54. The road was wider, but the houses looked the same, Playland at the Beach was gone now and replaced by a parking lot, but the couples walking along the beach seemed familiar. As we headed up the road to the Cliff House it seemed identical to walks I had taken nearly forty years ago. From the Cliff House we went inland and down the streets that Bill Talmadge had suggested. We even got lost once, but we arrived at the Golden Gate Bridge at three minutes past four on September seventh, 1990.

The hoopla and the foofooraw I had expected was not there. No one was there except Yvonne and I. There was no cameraman to record the sight for television around the nation. There was no one to interview me about my long walk home and no photographer to take my picture for the morning paper. Not even any Kiwanians to discuss my ordeal with and share in my experience. No key to the city and no congratulations from anyone!

I sat for a moment and looked at the bridge, a monument to the technical expertise of our society. I watched the tourists as they gawked at the bridge and photographed its beauty. My endeavor, my accomplishment was small in comparison to the magnificence of the bridge. The lack of anyone to share the trip with bothered me for a couple of minutes. This was not what I had led myself to expect.

After a minute or two of self pity I smiled to Yvonne, hugged her and said, "I did it. I walked from New York to San Francisco." She understood. I walked up to the bridge, wandered around for a while and then sat down on the grass to admire the beauty of the bridge, the bay and the day. I was also reveling in my accomplishment. I knew what I had done. I knew how much effort it took and I knew how I felt about it.

We stayed there for over an hour. The end of the trip was here and gone. Now we had to get to the hotel room. Bill Lacey, our Lieutenant governor from Atwater, had arranged a motel room, but first we had to get back to our car, eight miles away. I had walked far enough that I didn't want to walk back. Yvonne made it clear that she didn't want to walk back either, so I called a cab. After waiting a half an hour I called again. They said they were working on it. I didn't really believe it.

It seemed strange and somewhat ironic. After walking this far, we would have to walk eight miles back to the car. The idea that no one would be there at the conclusion except Yvonne had never occurred to me. The real world was never what I could imagine.

When I returned from the second call, Yvonne was talking to a very attractive young woman. When she heard what I was doing, she offered to drive us back to the car. We readily accepted.

Once at the car it was easy to drive to our motel. In the room, Operation KNOW had arranged for a bottle of red wine and a "Welcome" on the door. That evening the Director of the Kiwanis Foundation called me to congratulate me. Phil had arranged that. Yvonne and I went out to dinner, retired early and the next day headed back to Sonora.

As we drove home I thought about the people I had met across the country. I thought about the fine country we have and how diverse and fantastic it was. I recalled the long hours of walking and the miles of road that I had walked. It was a good walk.

My long walk home was complete. I had set a goal, planned it carefully and finally executed and completed it. I felt proud that I had done it and I was glad that it was over.

END

APPENDIX

Our Country

Any time I asked for help across this country, I was answered and answered very quickly and without any resentment. At no time did anyone ever bother me or even suggest they were going to bother me. We have a far finer country than what television displays. We have a far more caring country than the newspapers report. This is a fine strong country with caring and concerned people. I was glad to meet so many of them

Garbage

I walked a little over three thousand miles across the United States. The total trip was closer to thirty-seven hundred, but I took a few rides and a bus, so I walked a little over three thousand miles. I saw a lot of garbage along the roads, and I kept track of what I saw, statistically.

All the states I walked through had garbage. Some days there would be very little rubbish along the sides of the road. Other days there would be lots. Some states had volunteers to pick up the garbage, some used convicts, some paid workers for it. Some areas had churches and service groups clean up. The determining factor on garbage was time: how long since it was last picked up.

I expected beer cans and plastic bags, but there was a lot more along the roads. Below is a list of many of the things I saw.

Beer cans . . . . 52,158 cans.

The majority of the cans were Budweiser, Bud Dry or Bud Light. I expected Coors to overtake Bud in the west, but it never did, not even in Colorado.

Soft drink containers . 167,987 cans or bottles

In Pennsylvania and Ohio there was more Diet Pepsi than anything else. West of Indiana it was either Coke or Pepsi, with few diet drinks by the roads. Occasionally I would see Dr. Pepper or RC Cola in quantities above everything else, but this would only be for fifteen or twenty miles.

Bottle caps . . . . 249,842 caps

These were both the new plastic tops and the metal type. These had been tossed out of passing cars rather than stowing them in a garbage bag in the car.

Dead animals . . . . 732 road-kills

In Ohio and Missouri there were a lot of dead possums. In Illinois there were several dead rabbits. Turtles predominated in Pennsylvania. Also included in this number are fourteen deer, two cows, three sheep, five raccoons, two cats, seven dogs, eleven gray squirrels, twenty-five ground squirrels, six marmots and one antelope. Some of the dead animals had been dead for over a week. That made a walker walk faster.

Dead birds . . . . 4,724 dead birds

I did not expect to see dead birds, at least not in the quantity that I saw. Cardinals and canaries bothered me the most; they were such beautiful birds. There were a lot of sparrows and small black birds but only a few crows. There were twelve dead magpies. I found out the bills on the magpies in the east are white and those in California are yellow.

Insects . . . . . . about 156,800, most of them alive

In West Virginia and Ohio there were a lot of caterpillars trying to cross the road. In Kansas and Colorado there were grasshoppers. The majority of the insects were not dead, but scurrying along the side of the road. I'm sure there was a relationship between the number of insects and the number of dead birds. I noticed that the caterpillars in the east were predominantly green while those in Utah and Nevada were brown. Protective colorings?

Food wrappers . . . . . . 73,739 pieces of garbage

This consisted of bags, Styrofoam cartons, napkins and drink containers with company names. McDonald's predominated the garbage. In some areas Taco Bell would come close. It was easy to judge the distance to a fast food pit by the amount of their garbage on the road.

Tires . . . . 117 tires

Several of the tires were truck tires, discarded when a new one had to be put on. Since it was often difficult to get rid of old tires, they just left them at the side of the road. One tire was mounted on a rim and had probably fallen from the back of a pickup truck. It had been there long enough that it was flat.

Metal strips 247

These were primarily chrome plated strips from the sides of cars. They used to glue the chrome strips on the sides of cars. Sometimes the glue didn't hold. Some of the metal strips were aluminum. I had no idea where these came from.

Rubber cords 5,129

The majority of these were from trucks. This was most noticeable in Indiana, because the road I walked on in Indiana had a huge number of trucks. These 'bungie' cords were used to tie the canvas down on the top. When they broke, they fell off. Some of the straps were smaller ones from camper-trailers or tie-downs from the tops of the motor-homes. Very few had both ends on them. None of them were worth picking up.

Cigarette Packs ...... 12,941 packs

I hadn't even thought about cigarette packs being along the roads, but they were there. Marlboro predominated in most states. I expected that the number would decrease when I got to Utah, but it didn't. It remained relatively constant as compared to the number of cars on the road.

Money $5.21

I picked up $5.21 in change on the roads. This was three quarters, two in Pennsylvania and one in New Jersey, seven dimes, eighteen nickels and the rest in pennies. The majority of the money I found was in the first two weeks of walking. That was when my feet hurt and I was tired, so I was always looking down. Once I felt good, beginning about the third week, I was looking up, so I seldom saw any of the money on the ground, but I saw the birds flying and the trees and clouds. Near the end of the day I would occasionally see the coins. I considered them good luck, so I picked them up.

Keys .... 17 sets (mostly car keys)

Padlocks .... 7 locks (mostly combination)

Hand tools 27

I found one bent pair of pliers, five box end or open end wrenches, nine screw drivers, three lug wrenches, a set of Allen wrenches, a hacksaw, three hammers, a knife, a rubber mallet, a soldering iron and a wood chisel. Most of these were on outside curves where they had fallen off as the vehicles turned the corner.

Lug bolts 152

These are the nuts used to hold your rims on the car. I never saw more than one of these at a time that meant they probably came off and fell at the side of the road. Watch for cars with wobbly tires, they may be missing a few nuts to hold them on.

Ball point pens 87

The brand name on these was seldom readable. Most had been there for some time. None of them was worth keeping, or even picking up. There were also 37 broken pencils.

Caps 72

These were the baseball type hats with commercials on them. Most were stained and I didn't find any in good shape. They represented establishments such as Friendly Motors, New Holland Farm Machinery and Bar Ten Tavern.

Clothes . . . . 218 pieces

There were shirts, pants, shoes and socks. I saw three bras. One of the bras was lying in the gravel next to the letter 'Z' from a scrabble game. I wondered if they were put there together, and how. For the next few hours stories went through my mind on these two items together.

Disposable Diapers 2,142

I did not look to see how many of these disposable diapers contained number one and how many contained number two. It did bother me that they were there. Every time I saw a disposable diaper at the side of the road, I became concerned that the next car might decide to toss one out as it came by. The discarding of disposable diapers along the roadside represented to me one of the worst indicators of how we treat our roadsides.

Miscellaneous pieces of glass . . . . . lots
Miscellaneous pieces of rubber . . . lots
Miscellaneous pieces of paper . . . . lots
Miscellaneous pieces of metal . . . . lots
Miscellaneous pieces of plastic . . . lots

All along the roads were these pieces of crap, garbage from our lives. Some left from accidents, some fallen from vehicles unknowingly, most just tossed there because someone didn't want it anymore.

The worst thing about all this garbage at the side of our highways was that about eighty percent of it was intentionally put there with the idea that someone else will take care of my garbage. This was wrong; in most states it was illegal. We must accept the responsibility for our own garbage.

IF YOU WANT TO WALK

Loneliness: During the majority of the time you will be alone. If 'alone' means 'lonely' then don't try an extended walk. I found that time alone was one of the things that made my walk enjoyable. When I stayed in motels I did not turn on the television, I wanted the time to myself. I did carry a tape recorder, but only for recording my feelings and observations about my walk, not for listening to tapes.

Support: It helps a lot if you have some sort of a network to assist you along the roads. My suggestion is to join a local Kiwanis Club. When you do, mention, before you are inducted, that the reason you are joining Kiwanis is to get their support for your walk. If they know that you are not asking for money there should be no problem. They will generally give you addresses and phone numbers to assist you.

Pacing: You must remember that you are walking for enjoyment. If it's work, don't do it. If you are not having fun, go home. So walk at a pace that's comfortable, but demanding. Some days you will walk slower than other days. I went to my doctor before I left and took a tread-mill test. My doctor recommended that I not let my heart rate exceed one hundred forty beats per minute. He said for a brief period I was not to exceed one hundred fifty beats. When I carried a watch, I kept track of my heart rate. I did it often enough that when I didn't have a watch, I could estimate rather closely.

Your speed will also depend on the weight of your pack. Generally you can carry more when walking the roads than you can carry in the back country. The reason for this is the incline you would walk. In the back country your trails are often steep and you gain elevation in short distances. A gain of a thousand feet per mile is not unusual. Walking along the roads you will gain three hundred feet per mile. You can carry a heavier pack. In the back country the maximum weight of my pack is thirty-seven pounds. Along the roads the maximum weight of my pack was often forty-five pounds.

Another difference in walking roads as opposed to trails is what you see. When walking on trails, most of the time that you are moving, you are watching your feet., because the trail is not level. When walking on roads you don't watch your feet, you are able to look around and see the whole world. It is like window shopping on the roads of nature.

Equipment: My pack was old and not the best. I suggest you spend a lot of time with a knowledgeable person. Find a friend who has a back pack and ask to use it for a weekend. You will never find the perfect pack, but you will find one that is comfortable.

Shoes are a problem. Try reading Consumers Reports, July 1997. I was told that they recommend New Balance. I do too.

Itinerary

5/13 Sun	New York City
5/14 Mon	Union, NJ
5/15 Tue	Somerville, NJ
5/16 Wed	Lambertsville, NJ
5/17 Thu	New Hope, PA
5/18 Fri	Phoenixville, PA
5/19 Sat	Parkersburg, PA
5/20 Sun	Lancaster, PA
5/21 Mon	York, PA
5/22 Tue	Gettysberg, PA
5/23 Wed	Chambersburg
5/24 Thu	Ft. Laudon, PA
5/25 Fri	Somerset
5/26 Sat	Markleton, PA
5/27 Sun	Uniontown, PA
5/28 Mon	Waynesburg, PA
5/29 Tue	Hundred, WV
5/30 Wed	New Martinsville
5/31 Thur	St. Marys, WV
6/1 Fri	Belpre, OH
6/2 Sat	Athens, OH
6/3 Sun	McCarther, OH
6/4 Mon	Chillicothe, OH
6/5 Tue	Hillsboro, OH
6/6 Wed	Cincinnati, OH
6/7 Thu	Cincinnati, OH
6/8 Fri	Versailles, IN
6/9 Sat	Seymour, IN
6/10 Sun	Bedford, IN
6/11 Mon	Loogootee, IN
6/12 Tue	Lawrenceville, IL
6/13 Wed	Flora, IL
6/14 Thu	Salem, IL
6/15 Fri	Carlyle, IL
6/16 Sat	O'Fallon, IL

6/17 Sun	Gray Summit,MO
6/18 Mon	Union, MO
6/19 Tue	Owensville, MO
6/20 Wed	Owensville, MO
6/21 Thu	Belle, MO
6/22 Fri	Rolla, MO
6/23 Sat	St. Louis, MO
6/24 Sun	St. Louis, MO
6/25 Mon	St. Louis, MO
6/26 Tue	St. Louis, MO
6/27 Wed	St. Louis, MO
6/28 Thu	Nevada, MO
6/29 Fri	Ft. Scott, KS
6/30 Sat	Iola, KS
7/1 Sun	Eureka, KS
7/2 Mon	El Dorado, KS
7/3 Tue	Newton, KS
7/4 Wed	Hutchinson, KS
7/5 Thu	Lyons, KS
7/6 Fri	La Cross KS
7/7 Sat	Hays, KS
7/8 Sun	Colby, KS
7/9 Mon	Colby, KS
7/10 Tue	Goodland, KS
7/11 Wed	St. Francis, KS
7/12 Thu	Joes, CO
7/13 Fri	Anton, CO
7/14 Sat	bridge in CO
7/15 Sun	Strausburg, CO
7/16 Mon	Watkins, CO
7/17 Tue	Denver, CO
7/18 Wed	Greeley, CO
7/19 Thu	Loveland, CO
7/20 Fri	Estes Park, CO
7/21 Sat	Grand Lake, CO
7/22 Sun	Hot Sulphur, CO
7/23 Mon	Steamboat, CO
7/24 Tue	Craig, CO
7/25 Wed	Craig, CO
7/26 Thu	Craig, CO

7/27	Fri	Craig, CO
7/27	Fri	Meeker
7/28	Sat	Rifle, CO
7/29	Sun	Parachute, CO
7/30	Mon	Grand Junction
7/31	Tue	Grand Junction
8/1	Wed	Grand Junction
8/2	Thu	with Jo in Utah
8/3	Fri	with Jo in Utah
8/4	Sat	with Jo in Utah
8/5	Sun	Richfield, UT
8/6	Mon	Big Rock Candy
8/7	Tue	Junction, UT
8/8	Wed	Panguitch UT
8/9	Thu	Mt. Carmel, UT
8/10	Fri	Glendale, UT
8/11	Sat	Springdale, UT
8/12	Sun	Mt Carmel
8/13	Mon	Springdale, UT
8/14	Tue	St. George, UT
8/15	Wed	Las Vegas, NV
8/16	Thu	Culvert, NV
8/17	Fri	Lathrop WellsNV
8/18	Sat	Beatty, NV
8/19	Sun	Goldfield, NV
8/20	Mon	Tonapah, NV
8/21	Tue	Coaldale Jct, NV
8/22	Wed	Benton CA
8/23	Thur	Bishop, CA
8/24	Fri	Youth hostel, CA
8/25	Sat	June Lake, CA
8/26	Sun	Bridgeport, CA
8/27	Mon	Sonora Pass, CA
8/28	Tue	Strawberry, CA
8/29	Wed	Sonora, CA
8/30	Thu	Sonora, CA
8/31	Fri	Don Pedro, CA
9/1	Sat	Don Pedro, CA
9/2	Sun	Modesto, CA
9/3	Mon	E. Mt Hamilton

9/4 Tue	W. Mt Hamilton
9/5 Wed	San Jose, Ca
9/6 Thur	Redwood City
9/7 Fri	San Francisco

117 Days across the United States—3507 Miles

Names From The Trip

Chris Willis, Sloan, AR
Bob Gingrich, Oxford, AR
Herta Helm, Loidesthal, Austria
Irmgard Schiller,
   Fruhwirth, Vienna, Austria
Donna Phelps, Chandler, AZ
Delvin Thompson, Page, AZ
Dennis Wood, Phoenix, AZ
Theresa Kayona, Scottsdale, AZ
John Oechan, Sun Lakes, AZ
Gregory Davis, Atherton, CA
James H. Upton, Atherton, CA
Ed Abercrombie, Atwater, CA
Bob Kinman, Atwater, CA
Bill Lacey, Atwater, CA
Chuck McMahan, Atwater, CA
David Pettus, Benicia, CA
Candace Katosic, Big Oak Flat, CA
Tom Katosic, Big Oak Flat, CA
Ambroses Stone, Big Pines, CA
Thomas Stone, Big Pines, CA
Skip Quinn, Campbell, CA
Dale Cornelius, Cardiff, CA
Monika Frampton, Carmel, CA
Al Frampton, Carmel, CA
Shirley Mattingly, Clovis, CA
Clark Keefe, Colombia, CA
Birge Anthony, Columbia, CA
Betty Edwards, Columbia, CA
James Vanover, Columbia, CA
Robert Berwyn, Crowley Lake, CA
Cookie Jewel Aerie,
   Crowley Lake, CA
Sandy Jewel Aerie,
   Crowley Lake, CA
Sue Judson, Crowley Lake, CA
Leslie Oliver, Crowley Lake, CA
Jan Hull, Cupertino, CA

Richard L. Rea, Cupertino, CA
Michael Reynolds, Downey, CA
Darlene Azevedo, Fresno, CA
Val Dirlam, Fresno, CA
Michelle Gross, Fresno, CA
Kevin Gross, Fresno, CA
Karen Gross, Fresno, CA
Erich Gross, Fresno, CA
Shawna Hanlan, Fresno, CA
Vincent Bohleem, Garden Grove, CA
Phillip M. Lightly, Gilroy, CA
Skip Thomas, Groveland, CA
Ken Ginsalm, Healdsburg, CA
Edie Ginsalm, Healdsburg, CA
Diane Larrabee, Hermosa Beach, CA
Larry Larrabee, Hermosa Beach, CA
Louis Escobeds, Hesperia, CA
Cuelia Woods, Hesperia, CA
Opal Lawler, Independence, CA
Cindy Lawler, Independence, CA
Amber Lawler, Independence, CA
Pat Lawler, Independence, CA
Christain Lawler, Independence, CA
Ken Kram, Jamestown, CA
Kathy Madden, Jamestown, CA
Orv Millhollin, Jamestown, CA
Mel Williams, La Habra, CA
Homer Maertz, Laguna Hills, CA
Mary Lou Cooper, Los Altos, CA
Don Cooper, Los Altos, CA
Douglass M. Couch, Los Altos, CA
James W. Hodgen, Los Altos, CA
Ralph S. White, Los Altos, CA
Dody Moffat, Los Altos Hills, CA
H. Donald Winbigler,
   Los Altos Hills, CA
Phyllis Byrne, Los Angeles, CA
Pat Byrne, Los Angeles, CA

Homer A. Johnson, Mammoth, CA
Ken Moore, Mammoth, CA
Rodney Cogswell, Menlo Park, CA
William P. Gutgsell, Menlo Park, CA
Duncan L. Matteson,
    Menlo Park, CA
Dr. William M. Vaughan,
    Menlo Park, CA
Frank Taylor, Merced, CA
Ray Azevedo, Modesto, CA
Dorothy Azevedo, Modesto, CA
Sierra Hampton, Monterey, CA
Lee Brown, Morgan Hill, CA
Myrna Hampton, Monterey, CA
Gordon L. Furze,
    Mountain View, CA
J. Boyce Nute, Mountain View, CA
Mike Vangele, Mountain View, CA
John D. Woolridge,
    Mountain View, CA
Mark Amiot, Mt. Hamilton, CA
Cindy Barrett, Mt. Hamilton, CA
Eric Barrett, Mt. Hamilton, CA
Ron Barrett, Mt. Hamilton, CA
Billy Bernicchi, Mt. Hamilton, CA
Lynn Brown, Mt. Hamilton, CA
Doug Campbell, Mt. Hamilton, CA
Barbara Cook, Mt. Hamilton, CA
Gary Cook, Mt. Hamilton, CA
Glenna Dolfin, Mt. Hamilton, CA
Krystal Fisher, Mt. Hamilton, CA
David Garcia, Mt. Hamilton, CA
Bill Gehri, Mt. Hamilton, CA
Kelly Gehri, Mt. Hamilton, CA
Kevin Gehri, Mt. Hamilton, CA
Kortni Gehri, Mt. Hamilton, CA
Kristin Gehri, Mt. Hamilton, CA
Susie Gehri, Mt. Hamilton, CA
Gene Harlan, Mt. Hamilton, CA
Dave Lingo, Mt. Hamilton, CA

Kevin McCarthy, Mt. Hamilton, CA
Jill Owens, Mt. Hamilton, CA
Molly Owens, Mt. Hamilton, CA
Nick Owens, Mt. Hamilton, CA
Jack Schultz, Mt. Hamilton, CA
Sheri Schultz, Mt. Hamilton, CA
Jeremy Severinsen,
    Mt. Hamilton, CA
Sheryl Severinsen, Mt. Hamilton, CA
Logan Shankle, Mt. Hamilton, CA
Sam Shankle, Mt. Hamilton, CA
Susie Pharr, New Iberia, CA
Mark R. Pharr, New Iberia, CA
Kelly Spicer, Oxnard, CA
Richard Spicer, Oxnard, CA
Roberta Spicer, Oxnard, CA
Gael Owens, Pacific Grove, CA
Andy Anderson, Palo Alto, CA
Dr. Charles Arnold, Palo Alto, CA
Diane Avers, Palo Alto, CA
Charles P. Banovac, Palo Alto, CA
Paul H. Beveridge, Palo Alto, CA
Barbara Brown, Palo Alto, CA
Joseph G. Carleton, Palo Alto, CA
R. Bernard Coley, Palo Alto, CA
Claude C. Davis, Palo Alto, CA
Richard F. Douglas, Palo Alto, CA
Mark Greenstein, Palo Alto, CA
Elster S. Haile, Palo Alto, CA
John P. Hanna, Palo Alto, CA
Elmer Hawkins, Palo Alto, CA
Michael J. Irvin, Palo Alto, CA
Donna Jang, Palo Alto, CA
Lynn Johnson, Palo Alto, CA
Paul W. Madsen, Palo Alto, CA
N. Patricia McGuire, Palo Alto, CA
Elie Monarch, Palo Alto, CA
Donald E. Peterson, Palo Alto, CA
Henry Ponleithner, Palo Alto, CA
William E. Reller, Palo Alto, CA

Charles Ridley, Palo Alto, CA
Luther A. Rogerson, Palo Alto, CA
Ray P. Ruppel, Palo Alto, CA
Julius E. Schuchat, Palo Alto, CA
Sheldon Solloway, Palo Alto, CA
Dr. James D. Stephens,
    Palo Alto, CA
Rick Stern, Palo Alto, CA
Nate Titterton, Palo Alto, CA
Bert Torres, Palo Alto, CA
William F. Van Orsdol, Palo Alto, CA
Craig Yates, Palo Alto, CA
Kay McGill, Point Richmond, CA
Dorothy Bradshaw,
    Portola Valley, CA
Jerry Berens,
    Rancho Palos Verdes, CA
Warren J. Merritt, Redding, CA
Roy Klebe, Redwood City, CA
Joseph R. Payne, Redwood City, CA
Miles Saunders, Sacramento, CA
Kit Tyler, Sacramento, CA
Cathy O'Brien, San Bernadino, CA
Ray O'Brien, San Bernadino, CA
Leni Lane, San Carlos, CA
James Agate, San Francisco, CA
Officer William Dodds,
    San Francisco, CA
J. Gordon Dowsett,
    San Francisco, CA
John Hanley, San Francisco, CA
Robin Okoneski, San Francisco, CA
Bill Talmage, San Francisco, CA
Laurie Valencia, San Francisco, CA
Wayne Augsburger, San Jose, CA
G.G. Ballard, San Jose, CA
Bill Bartley, San Jose, CA
Bill Beck, San Jose, CA
Ted Becker, San Jose, CA
Don Bell, San Jose, CA

Ken Bryant, San Jose, CA
Richard Buchner, San Jose, CA
Steve Coons, San Jose, CA
Kathi Corya, San Jose, CA
Stephen Ferry, San Jose, CA
Steve Ferry, San Jose, CA
Gary Frazier, San Jose, CA
Dick Gardner, San Jose, CA
Larry Giuffre, San Jose, CA
Ron Gregg, San Jose, CA
Steve Hailes, San Jose, CA
Ray Hamilton, San Jose, CA
Marty Hatzke, San Jose, CA
Ralph J. Hendrickson, San Jose, CA
Mike Hernandez, San Jose, CA
Steve Howard, San Jose, CA
James Jimenez-Sullivan,
    San Jose, CA
Martha Kelly, San Jose, CA
Joe Ketner, San Jose, CA
Charlie King, San Jose, CA
Bob Koelho, San Jose, CA
James Lucarotti, San Jose, CA
Larry Lupo, San Jose, CA
Jim Marcelli, San Jose, CA
Ted Marfia, San Jose, CA
Joe Marty, San Jose, CA
Jim McRhoads, San Jose, CA
Jas. Douglas Moffat, San Jose, CA
Don Perera, San Jose, CA
Fred Peterson, San Jose, CA
John Redding, San Jose, CA
Bill Ress, San Jose, CA
Jackie Rose, San Jose, CA
Theresa Smith, San Jose, CA
Jack Squires, San Jose, CA
Dennis Nelson, San Leandro, CA
Angie Frabasilie, San Rafael, CA
Coleen Curran, Santa Clara, CA
Sam Kattuah, Santa Clara, CA

Marilian Lewis, Santa Clara, CA
Mary Webster, Sepulveda, CA
David Webster, Sepulveda, CA
Kurt Mayer, Simi Valley, CA
Susan Gonzalez-Ross,
    Simi Valley, CA
Hedy Wood, Soulsbyville, CA
Ellis Adcock, Sonora, CA
Greg Applegate, Sonora, CA
Bud Baker, Sonora, CA
Betty Baker, Sonora, CA
Dale Batchelor, Sonora, CA
Chris Bateman, Sonora, CA
Hal Bomgardner, Sonora, CA
Mort Bonnell, Sonora, CA
Ruth Bonnell, Sonora, CA
Marijuel Borges, Sonora, CA
Bill Boyd, Sonora, CA
Dorothy Brown, Sonora, CA
Jim Brown, Sonora, CA
Pat Bumpus, Sonora, CA
Dan Calvert, Sonora, CA
Clyde Caya, Sonora, CA
Peter Cheney, Sonora, CA
Sue Clark, Sonora, CA
Smokey Cole, Sonora, CA
Bill Craig, Sonora, CA
Don Dambacher, Sonora, CA
Paul Davis, Sonora, CA
Jackie Davis, Sonora, CA
Michael Dolan, Sonora, CA
Harlan Dunning, Sonora, CA
Trudy Dunning, Sonora, CA
Paul Durbee, Sonora, CA
Buzz Eggleston, Sonora, CA
Karen Eggleton, Sonora, CA
Carole Elder, Sonora, CA
Cassle Elder, Sonora, CA
Walt Emig, Sonora, CA
Wilma Emig, Sonora, CA

Pete Falger, Sonora, CA
Chuck Giordano, Sonora, CA
Tammy Gleason, Sonora, CA
Ron Gluiso, Sonora, CA
J.B. Harmon, Sonora, CA
Gyle Harmon, Sonora, CA
Larry Hashman, Sonora, CA
Joy Henibree, Sonora, CA
Danny Heuton, Sonora, CA
Will Hodges, Sonora, CA
John Hoffman, Sonora, CA
George Holman, Sonora, CA
Dori Hopper, Sonora, CA
Frank Jackson, Sonora, CA
Bill Kaiser, Sonora, CA
Marie Kasak, Sonora, CA
Barbara Kay, Sonora, CA
Ron Knox, Sonora, CA
Larry Kram, Sonora, CA
Joycie Lopez, Sonora, CA
Diane Malstrom, Sonora, CA
Beckie Manin, Sonora, CA
Jessie Manugueria, Sonora, CA
John Matthews, Sonora, CA
Yvonne Mattingly, Sonora, CA
Marcie McCulouch, Sonora, CA
Harvey C. McGee, Sonora, CA
Kieth McKenzie, Sonora, CA
Lois McLain, Sonora, CA
Sandra Mildenberger, Sonora, CA
Allen Miller, Sonora, CA
Lynne Miller, Sonora, CA
Chris Miller, Sonora, CA
Ed Minium, Sonora, CA
Leo Mitsopoules, Sonora, CA
Pat Neeley, Sonora, CA
Tim Neeley, Sonora, CA
Dick Nutting, Sonora, CA
Leetta Nutting, Sonora, CA
Tony Pallante, Sonora, CA

Joe Palumbo, Sonora, CA
Carleton Penwell, Sonora, CA
Ros Roberts, Sonora, CA
Larry Rotelli, Sonora, CA
Jack Rucker, Sonora, CA
Phil Sandoval, Sonora, CA
Lola Sandoval, Sonora, CA
George Segarini, Sonora, CA
Judy Smith, Sonora, CA
Rex Spaith, Sonora, CA
Carley Steichen, Sonora, CA
Laura Steichen, Sonora, CA
Ron Stern, Sonora, CA
Arnie Stradinger, Sonora, CA
Angie Thomas, Sonora, CA
Paul Tighe, Sonora, CA
Connie Tighe, Sonora, CA
Dan Townsend, Sonora, CA
Jo Vargo, Sonora, CA
Hank Vienop, Sonora, CA
Bud Vogel, Sonora, CA
Wally Wirtz, Sonora, CA
Peggy Zuber, Sonora, CA
Fredric O. Glover, Stanford, CA
Mark Johnstone, Sunnyvale, CA
Celest Adams, Temecula, CA
Celeste Adams, Temecula, CA
Bev Stone, Temecula, CA
Bev Stone, Temecula, CA
Sue Brown, Three Rivers, CA
Willie Treece, Three Rivers, CA
Little Willie Treece,
    Three Rivers, CA
Emily Treece, Three Rivers, CA
Bobbie Treece, Three Rivers, CA
Diane Treece, Three Rivers, CA
Joe Bonnello, Trabuco Canyon, CA
Phillis Fuentes, Tuolumne, CA
Koney Bowmaster, Tuolumne, CA
Steve Patton, Tuolumne, CA

Jack Amason, Turlock, CA
Yvonne Amason, Turlock, CA
Dr. Robert Clark, Turlock, CA
Marlene Broddy, Twain Harte, CA
Ron Core, Twain Harte, CA
Bill Craig, Twain Harte, CA
Ed Larsen, Twain Harte, CA
LeRoy Tuttle, Twain Harte, CA
Pat McCloskey, Victorville, CA
Jim Caviglia, Visalia, CA
Jerry Hornig, Wawawona, CA
Lee Boglar, Winton, CA
Deanna Beare, Woo, CA
Chuck Heller, Yreka, CA
Shane Lundgren,
    Calgary, Alberta, Canada
Don Myers,
    Calgary, Alberta, Canada
Steve Healy,
    Calgary, Alberta, Canada
Sruart Myers,
    Calgary, Alberta, Canada
Neil Bertholf, Arvada, CO
Craig Chapel, Arvada, CO
Rita Iannuzzi, Arvada, CO
Dennis Iannuzzi, Arvada, CO
Pete Iannuzzi, Arvada, CO
Denise Iannuzzi, Arvada, CO
Robert L. Bradford, Aurora, CO
Ruth Bradford, Aurora, CO
Dave Howe, Aurora, CO
Sue Howe, Aurora, CO
Rick Shelbourn, Bennet, CO
Linda Willison, Bennett, CO
Kandace Donovan, Boulder, CO
Liz Gaggini, Boulder, CO
Karen L. Gesar, Boulder, CO
Benjamin Gesar, Boulder, CO
Neal R. Greenberg, Boulder, CO
Kate Kelly Grenger, Boulder, CO

Lynne Mattingly, Boulder, CO
Matthew Provost, Boulder, CO
Alexander Rigden, Boulder, CO
Chris Swan, Boulder, CO
Mark Shaw, Colorado Springs, CO
Allen Blanchard, Craig, CO
Thomas Boyd, Craig, CO
Mike Brinks, Craig, CO
Joe Chivington, Craig, CO
Chris Cooper, Craig, CO
Jeff Corriveay, Craig, CO
Don Cronk, Craig, CO
Steve Deto, Craig, CO
Genevieve Edwards, Craig, CO
Joe Edwards, Craig, CO
Rick Eversale, Craig, CO
Steve Grandboucke, Craig, CO
Rocky Innes, Craig, CO
Howard H. Kling, Craig, CO
Bill Lawrence, Craig, CO
Gary Loyd, Craig, CO
Fred E. Mason, Craig, CO
Neil McCandless, Craig, CO
Butch McKune, Craig, CO
Gary W. Nall, Craig, CO
Julie Nall, Craig, CO
Roy F. Nitschke, Craig, CO
Pete Pleasant, Craig, CO
Sid Pleasant, Craig, CO
C.F. Rakestraw, Craig, CO
Arnold Ridder, Craig, CO
Mildred Okes Rogers, Craig, CO
Merel Rogers, Craig, CO
Len Schnerdy, Craig, CO
Larry Seip, Craig, CO
Joe Self, Craig, CO
Avis Self, Craig, CO
Dennis Shannon, Craig, CO
Jim 'Harive' Shepperd, Craig, CO
Max Sims, Craig, CO

Delores Adamek St. Louis, Craig, CO
Sinclair St. Louis, Craig, CO
Joy Tayyaro, Craig, CO
Tom Trevenen, Craig, CO
Fred Trouth, Craig, CO
Douglas Virgil, Craig, CO
Dushan Voyuh, Craig, CO
Dave Zachley, Craig, CO
Bruce Zobel, Craig, CO
Jane ?, Denver, CO
John Archibald, Denver, CO
Rod Ellerbusch, Denver, CO
Shannon Faulhaber, Denver, CO
Laura Gaggini, Denver, CO
Paul Gaggini, Denver, CO
Cary L. Goodman, Denver, CO
Jim Hughes, Denver, CO
Joe Lake, Denver, CO
Dean Medina, Denver, CO
Dan Palermo, Denver, CO
Raymond Shaw, Denver, CO
Barbara Shaw, Denver, CO
Al Keeler, Englewood, CO
Dick Anema, Estes Park, CO
Paul Pirnat, Estes Park, CO
Betty Fischer, Fort Collins, CO
Julin Eisenbery, Ft Collins, CO
Harold Wilken, Ft Collins, CO
Oliver Wilken, Ft Collins, CO
Susanne Beauregard, Ft. Collins, CO
Joe Crilain, Ft. Collins, CO
Ralph Crillo, Ft. Collins, CO
Orion Hajard, Ft. Collins, CO
Art Jackson, Ft. Collins, CO
Casey Farrell, Granby, CO
Michael Farrell, Granby, CO
Rhonda Farrell, Granby, CO
Kelly Farrell, Granby, CO
Trooper R.L. Taylor, Granby, CO

Jim Aguilera, Grand Junction, CO
Jill Aguilera, Grand Junction, CO
Bonnie Armsby, Grand Junction, CO
John Bacheldor, Grand Junction, CO
Larry Ball, Grand Junction, CO
Velma Bilger, Grand Junction, CO
Wally Bissinger, Grand Junction, CO
Theresa Bouley, Grand Junction, CO
Jacque Chappell-Reid,
  Grand Junction, CO
Bob Colony, Grand Junction, CO
Ted Crawford, Grand Junction, CO
Jeff Cyriacks, Grand Junction, CO
Glen Davis, Grand Junction, CO
Brent Dawson, Grand Junction, CO
Richard Emerson,
  Grand Junction, CO
Al Gibbs, Grand Junction, CO
Norm Gifford, Grand Junction, CO
Dale C. Hardy, Grand Junction, CO
Andrea Heath, Grand Junction, CO
Toni Lou Heiden,
  Grand Junction, CO
Bill Holme, Grand Junction, CO
E. Bruce Isaaozia,
  Grand Junction, CO
Earl Jensen, Grand Junction, CO
Pete Jouflas, Grand Junction, CO
Jorn Moore, Grand Junction, CO
Steve Morrison, Grand Junction, CO
Bryant Nisley, Grand Junction, CO
Louie Paretti, Grand Junction, CO
Earl F. Payne, Grand Junction, CO
Bruce L. Penny,
  Grand Junction, CO
Harry Pforzheumer, Jr.,
  Grand Junction, CO
Tom Piper, Grand Junction, CO
Karen Ann Seidel,
  Grand Junction, CO

Friderick Stantug,
  Grand Junction, CO
Wayne Thaler, Grand Junction, CO
Jay Tolman, Grand Junction, CO
Rose Tomlinson, Grand Junction, CO
Herman Vorbech, Grand Junction, CO
Jim Wagner, Grand Junction, CO
Bill Waldeck, Grand Junction, CO
Jo Waldeck, Grand Junction, CO
Kathy Waters, Grand Junction, CO
Jack Wilhous, Grand Junction, CO
Lynn Wilson, Grand Junction, CO
Lee Young, Grand Junction, CO
Nicole Jensen, Grand Lake, CO
Cassie Lanz, Grand Lake, CO
Michael Moore, Grand Lake, CO
Joe Adstral, Greeley, CO
Vic Alcazar, Greeley, CO
Bob Anderson, Greeley, CO
Loreb Barttell, Greeley, CO
Barbara Blomeyer, Greeley, CO
Mark Brown, Greeley, CO
Candy Bryan, Greeley, CO
Craig Carlson, Greeley, CO
Chloe Childresa, Greeley, CO
Julie Coy, Greeley, CO
Bill Crews, Greeley, CO
B.T. 'Dan' Daniels, Greeley, CO
Joyce Ehrlich, Greeley, CO
Red Flannelly, Greeley, CO
Rosemary Fri, Greeley, CO
Dr. Andy Gibbons, Greeley, CO
Korie Goodman, Greeley, CO
Gregor Halenda, Greeley, CO
Dale Hall, Greeley, CO
Tom Harrison, Greeley, CO
Bill Hillard, Greeley, CO
Mark Hinze, Greeley, CO
Sam Hofer, Greeley, CO
Kermit Huckabay, Greeley, CO

Jim Huff, Greeley, CO
Bob Husmann, Greeley, CO
Harold Jones, Greeley, CO
Kary Karchmer, Greeley, CO
Leeann Karchmer, Greeley, CO
Stan Kerns, Greeley, CO
Bernard Kinnick, Greeley, CO
Roky Kron, Greeley, CO
Will Kulp, Greeley, CO
Les Langford, Greeley, CO
Mel Leedom, Greeley, CO
Sandy Linscome, Greeley, CO
Bob Lynch, Greeley, CO
Frank Martinez, Greeley, CO
Richard Maxfield, Greeley, CO
Chuck Meyers, Greeley, CO
Warren Mitchell, Greeley, CO
Jo Ann Mitchell, Greeley, CO
Stuart Mitchell, Greeley, CO
Don Neece, Greeley, CO
Richard Redfern, Greeley, CO
Lou Rieker, Greeley, CO
Trudance Anne Roberts, Greeley, CO
John Rutledge, Greeley, CO
Al Slighter, Greeley, CO
Tom Smith, Greeley, CO
Kent Stauffer, Greeley, CO
Ken Storck, Greeley, CO
Sue Swartz, Greeley, CO
Vanesa Tdahlynn Karre, Greeley, CO
Gary Tdahlynn Karre, Greeley, CO
Merideth Tdahlynn Karre,
    Greeley, CO
Ray Ulibarri, Greeley, CO
Mike Usher, Greeley, CO
Jim Vounieal, Greeley, CO
Ralph Waldo, Greeley, CO
Robert Waldo, Greeley, CO
Steve Walter, Greeley, CO
Gwen Willburn, Greeley, CO

Mike Winberry, Greeley, CO
Wally Birlew, Gypsum, CO
Brian Roberica,
    Highlands Ranch, CO
Abraham Rodridgus,
    Hot Sulphur Springs, CO
Paul K. Peters, Idalia, CO
Lou Sharpe, Joes, CO
Glen Sharpe, Joes, CO
Ray Flieger, Lakewood, CO
Randy Temple, Littleton, CO
Dave Knowlton, Longmont, CO
Ron Burke, Loveland, CO
Tim Businger, Loveland, CO
William Cairns, Loveland, CO
Dave Davidson, Loveland, CO
Dave Dubois, Loveland, CO
Steve Everell, Loveland, CO
Don Ford, Loveland, CO
Kiut L. Gersch, Loveland, CO
Betty Hedgespeth, Loveland, CO
Ron Hedgespeth, Loveland, CO
Forrest S. Knox, Loveland, CO
Mike Olexrdes, Loveland, CO
Dick Rogus, Loveland, CO
Roger Schulz, Loveland, CO
Sharon Spoon, Loveland, CO
Ralph Strar, Loveland, CO
Gaylen Williamson, Loveland, CO
Leo Wotan, Loveland, CO
Andrea Wotan, Loveland, CO
Jim Cook, Meeker, CO
Jan Hughley, Meeker, CO
Herb Hughley, Meeker, CO
Bill Ockhart, Mesa, CO
Bob L. Arnett, Parachute, CO
David Croley, Parachute, CO
Pauline Rosten, Parachute, CO
Claudette Birlew, Rifle, CO
Gloria Buchhewster, Rifle, CO

Bruce A. Jewell, Rifle, CO
Dale Kivisto, Rifle, CO
Bob Archer, Rulison, CO
Kassandra Archer, Rulison, CO
Kristen Wright, Rulison, CO
Kris Wright, Rulison, CO
Josh Wright, Rulison, CO
Doug Bostrom,
　Steamboat Springs, CO
Mel Braley, Steamboat Springs, CO
Al Brock, Steamboat Springs, CO
Robert Burks,
　Steamboat Springs, CO
Ed Daw, Steamboat Springs, CO
Dan Ellison, Steamboat Springs, CO
Jeremy Glaisher,
　Steamboat Springs, CO
Michael King,
　Steamboat Springs, CO
Mike Loth, Steamboat Springs, CO
Patrick McCosh,
　Steamboat Springs, CO
Nick Rose, Steamboat Springs, CO
Jim Severson,
　Steamboat Springs, CO
Dr. Pinky Smith,
　Steamboat Springs, CO
Carl Vail, Steamboat Springs, CO
Jan Vail, Steamboat Springs, CO
Mark Vige, Steamboat Springs, CO
Mario C. Virgil,
　Steamboat Springs, CO
Scott Welles, Steamboat Springs, CO
David Williams,
　Steamboat Springs, CO
Jim Winter, Steamboat Springs, CO
Marsha Bogolin, Strasberg, CO
Bill Crosman, Strasberg, CO
Tom Crouch, Strasberg, CO
Mary Dpbyns, Strasberg, CO

Randy Dpbyns, Strasberg, CO
George Nikel, Strasberg, CO
James I. Langford, Thornton, CO
Eleanor Rice, Watkins, CO
Meg Chaloupka, Windsor, CO
Rod Kehmeier, Windsor, CO
Jim Puth, Windsor, CO
Melvin Whipple, Windsor, CO
Katie Wales, Stamford, CT
Jim Harris, Torrington, CT
Tom Giblin, Washington, DC
Katherine 'Katie',
　Shulman, Washington, DC
Jerry Shulman, Washington, DC
Victoria Shulman, Washington, DC
Judy Shulman, Washington, DC
Alfo Emersleben,
　Geidingsa, East Germany
Peter Klim, Deerfield Beach, FL
Gricell Co, Deerfield Beach, FL
Elise Gichon, Hollywood, FL
Mish Decic, Lighthouse Point, FL
Dede Wortendyke, Pinellas Park, FL
E.H. "Bud" Wortendyke,
　Pinellas Park, FL
Phyllis A. Cloman, Pinellas Park, FL
Phillippa Holtz, ?, France
Xanier Chevrel, ?, France
Bob Jackson, Griffin, GA
E.W. Chastain, Kennesaw, GA
Norma Falco, Lilburn, GA
Mike Falco, Lilburn, GA
Anne Pitts, Lilburn, GA
Jim Dawson, Marietta, GA
Brent Hill, Marietta, GA
Darlene Oberle, Marietta, GA
Jack Prather, Marietta, GA
Steve Leegow, Marietta, GA
Marianne Smith, Thomatton, GA
Philip Gold, Woodstack, GA

Kim Sonderholm,
  Greve Strand, Germany
Kristian Sonderholm,
  Greve Strand, Germany
Karina Sonderholm,
  Greve Strand, Germany
Stefau Wernfurtuce,
  Pichlmaysh, Germany
Oliver Hill, Worms, Germany
Burs Vanbeek, Holland
Reqren Vanbeek, Holland
Dick H. Vanbeek, Holland
Eryka A. Long, Mtn. Home, ID
Belinda P. Long, Mtn. Home, ID
Gleason W. Long, Mtn. Home, ID
Jennifer M. Long, Mtn. Home, ID
Cristina D. Long, Mtn. Home, ID
Danald Cullinor, Albion, IL
Donald Walker, Alton, IL
Warren D. Carson, Belleville, IL
Paul Berndsen, Breeze, IL
Nickolas Hacchiarol, Breeze, IL
Clayton Mitchell, Carlyle, IL
Cathy Norman, Carlyle, IL
Jim Parrish, Chicago, IL
Calvin Schaffer, Chicago, IL
Vic Ackerson, Flora, IL
Don Buts, Flora, IL
Dominic Cricelli, Flora, IL
Bill Cunningham, Flora, IL
Buol Doud, Flora, IL
Robert E. Ellis, Flora, IL
Donald Evans, Flora, IL
Charlie Overstreet, Flora, IL
Barney Steele, Flora, IL
Jamis I. Waldby, Flora, IL
Bill Holshouser, Highland, IL
Bob Hoskins, Highland, IL
Wally Hug, Highland, IL
Milton Steiner, Highland, IL

Joe W. Garrison, Lawrenceville, IL
John L. Harris, Lawrenceville, IL
Larry Herron, Lawrenceville, IL
Michael Herron, Lawrenceville, IL
Bob Moor, Lawrenceville, IL
Kenneth Phillips, Lawrenceville, IL
Mervin Rosborough,
  Lawrenceville, IL
Roosevelt Bennett, Lebanon, IL
Yvette Jensen, Lebanon, IL
Bill Monroe, Lebanon, IL
Jerry Baily, Louisville, IL
Gary Ravlik, Manchester, IL
Lafe Berberich, Mt. Carmel, IL
Luicla Brown, Olney, IL
Allen Elliot, Olney, IL
Vickie Gagnon, Olney, IL
Donald Royse, Olney, IL
Tony Trotter, Olney, IL
Becky ?, O'Fallon, IL
Laura ?, O'Fallon, IL
Warren D. Carson, O'Fallon, IL
Dick Erlmann, O'Fallon, IL
Denise Farley, O'Fallon, IL
Clyde W. Glenn, O'Fallon, IL
Gene Jones, O'Fallon, IL
Kim Kardaver, O'Fallon, IL
Ray Kuykendall, O'Fallon, IL
Dareus G. Monson, O'Fallon, IL
Ann Moser, O'Fallon, IL
Don Moser, O'Fallon, IL
Gary Moser, O'Fallon, IL
Paul Owens, O'Fallon, IL
Earl Powe, O'Fallon, IL
Karen Powe, O'Fallon, IL
David Weatherford, O'Fallon, IL
Becky Zotz, O'Fallon, IL
Janet Park, Pawnee, IL
Jean Marliere, Peoria, IL
Donna Sidwell, Peoria, IL

Russell Fanction, Robinson, IL
Larry Wiseman, Robinson, IL
Tom Wiseman, Robinson, IL
Richard Whittaker, Sumner, IL
Andrew Niederberger, Swansen, IL
Jerry Drummond, Toledo, IL
John Kendall, Watttoon, IL
Kimberly West, Batesville, IN
Vernon Adams, Bedford, IN
Joan Adams, Bedford, IN
Billie Agnew, Bedford, IN
Elezabeth Buttz, Bedford, IN
John R. Buttz, Bedford, IN
Dave Cholgee, Bedford, IN
Ron Graulen, Bedford, IN
Shana Helsly, Bedford, IN
Joe Henley, Bedford, IN
Jerry Loveland, Bedford, IN
Judy Reynolds, Bedford, IN
Amy Sailor, Bedford, IN
Maxine Sullican, Bedford, IN
Travis Tanants, Bedford, IN
Frances Tanants, Bedford, IN
Ambra Kellen, Bicknell, IN
Joshua Kellen, Bicknell, IN
Jim Kellen, Bicknell, IN
Darlene Kellen, Bicknell, IN
Jeremy Kellen, Bicknell, IN
Andy Watkins, Bicknell, IN
Bill Bill Watkins, Bicknell, IN
Chris Cockerham, Brownstown, IN
Chris Cockerham, Brownstown, IN
Doanalo Cox, Brownstown, IN
James Marshall, Brownstown, IN
Shawn M. Patterson, Brownstown, IN
Shannon Daaco, Columbus, IN
Sue Keathley, East Oolitic, IN
Mona Floyd, Elrod, IN
Pat West, Glendora, IN
Russ Schirtz, Goshen, IN

Pat Black, Indianapolis, IN
Joel Hedge, Indianapolis, IN
Nathan Snell, Indianapolis, IN
Julie Grubough, Laotto, IN
Don Grubough, Laotto, IN
Larry Brewer, Lawrenceberg, IN
Michael Williams, Lawrenceberg, IN
Bebee Blair, Loogootee, IN
Robert C. Enlow, Loogootee, IN
Larry Long, Loogootee, IN
Afra Mauder, Loogootee, IN
Glen Nolan, Loogootee, IN
Jr. Salman, Loogootee, IN
Grey Salman, Loogootee, IN
Rich Summers, Loogootee, IN
Randy Barlay, Medora, IN
Missy Guthrie, Medora, IN
Brendz Guthrie, Medora, IN
Tommy F. Gordon, Milan, IN
Sharon Gordon, Milan, IN
U. L. Capehart, Mitchell, IN
Ken Teegen, Mitchell, IN
Denise Delany, Montgomery, IN
Amos H. Miller, Montgomery, IN
Mary Wagler, Montgomery, IN
Martha Wittmer, Montgomery, IN
H. Joe Maschlin, North Vernon, IN
James Mullins, North Vernon, IN
Tush Refrer, North Vernon, IN
Edna Rocky, North Vernon, IN
Perry Sands, North Vernon, IN
David Berryman, Pleasantville, IN
Jack Slunder, Princeton, IN
Donna Fish, Richmand, IN
Bill Fish, Richmand, IN
Ralph Allen, Seymour, IN
Tom Ross, Seymour, IN
Jim Rsstrelle, Seymour, IN
Jeff Wkay, Seymour, IN
Andrea Deckard, Shoals, IN

Tim Vogel, Shoals, IN
Diana White, Shoals, IN
Tita Wyman, Shoals, IN
Junior Smith, Sidia, IN
Joshua Smith, Sidia, IN
Andrea Dluguy, South Bend, IN
Charlie Allen, Versales, IN
Terry A. Black, Versales, IN
Lyman P. Conley, Versales, IN
Everett Elston, Versales, IN
Jim Evans, Versales, IN
Ed Krause, Versales, IN
Wayne Martin, Versales, IN
Timmy Martin, Versales, IN
David Martin, Versales, IN
William Nunn, Versales, IN
John Oz, Versales, IN
Pat Shakey, Versales, IN
Jess Westmeyer, Versales, IN
Bob Brown, Vincennes, IN
David Culp, Vincennes, IN
David Dely, Vincennes, IN
Patty Holscher, Vincennes, IN
Loiann Irving, Vincennes, IN
Mike Johnson, Vincennes, IN
Belle Kasting, Vincennes, IN
Debbie Leonard, Vincennes, IN
George McCormack, Vincennes, IN
Bob Pfoff, Vincennes, IN
Helen Pfoff, Vincennes, IN
Paul R. Sweeney, Vincennes, IN
Bill Watkins, Vincennes, IN
Dale Wirth, Vincennes, IN
Marion Barber, Washington, IN
Mary Barber, Washington, IN
Hugh F. Billings, Washington, IN
Fred Blair, Washington, IN
John Keller, Washington, IN
Amos Lindsey, Washington, IN
Bill McCain, Washington, IN

Martin L. Mumaw III,
  Washington, IN
Mike Neff, Washington, IN
Nona Oesterle, Washington, IN
Steve Pershing, Washington, IN
Rev. Lyle Rasmussen,
  Washington, IN
Jeff Scott, Washington, IN
Alice Shanks, Washington, IN
Mary Shanks, Washington, IN
Nancy Solliday, Washington, IN
Terry L. Wise, Washington, IN
Robert D. Slater, Etshell, IN
Albert Wilkins, Kalona, IO
Bellet Renato, Torino, Italy
Ghiglione Armando, Voghera, Italy
Thelma Gray, Americus, KS
Ruben Bruntz, Bazine, KS
Kathy Meyers, Bucyrus, KS
Tom Meyers, Bucyrus, KS
Dorothy Garlick,
  Buffalo Corners, KS
Duane R. Garlick,
  Buffalo Corners, KS
Creighton S. Smith, Butler Co, KS
Greg Bartell, Colby, KS
Steve Bell, Colby, KS
Steve Bixenman, Colby, KS
Star Britt, Colby, KS
R. Darlina, Colby, KS
Mary James, Colby, KS
Tom Levit, Colby, KS
Stan Molstad, Colby, KS
Jari Skiles, Colby, KS
Randy Wilson, Colby, KS
Lilian Branin, Coyvill, KS
John W. Greer, Coyvill, KS
Alice Greer, Coyvill, KS
Hill Wilmare, Coyvill, KS
John Anderson, El Dorado, KS

Larry Baker, El Dorado, KS
Stace Barker, El Dorado, KS
Kenneth C. Burgert, El Dorado, KS
Janet G. Chapman, El Dorado, KS
Cathy Cooper, El Dorado, KS
Eunice Faulconer, El Dorado, KS
Richard Faulconer, El Dorado, KS
Guy H. Faulconer, El Dorado, KS
Amy Graham, El Dorado, KS
Tamara Gusip, El Dorado, KS
John Harstine, El Dorado, KS
Charlie E. Heilmann, El Dorado, KS
David Kopsia, El Dorado, KS
Sean Patty, El Dorado, KS
Wilfred Pettus, El Dorado, KS
Ben Plummer, El Dorado, KS
Jean Plummer, El Dorado, KS
Bob Reed, El Dorado, KS
Mary Reed, El Dorado, KS
Jess Reed, El Dorado, KS
Harold S. Smith, El Dorado, KS
Vic Thomison, El Dorado, KS
Dana Thomison, El Dorado, KS
Art Thomison, El Dorado, KS
Leon White, El Dorado, KS
Kate Peters, Eminence, KS
Joy Peters, Eminence, KS
Ralph Janssen, Erie, KS
Dicy Janssen, Erie, KS
Jim Bagnell, Eureka, KS
Bruce C. Detwiler, Eureka, KS
Roy L. Donaldson, Eureka, KS
Raymond Filumne, Eureka, KS
Mayor James H. Francis, Eureka, KS
Tom Grooms, Eureka, KS
John Huntington, Eureka, KS
Dwight Huntington, Eureka, KS
Nancy Huntington, Eureka, KS
Grant Moody, Eureka, KS
Evan Moody, Eureka, KS

Sheryl Moody, Eureka, KS
Jonathan Moody, Eureka, KS
Mike Moody, Eureka, KS
Stacie Sanders, Eureka, KS
Mary Lynn Cartwright, Ft. Scott, KS
Shelly L. Littleton-Sanborn,
   Ft. Scott, KS
Juanita Monroe, Ft. Scott, KS
Del Potter, Ft. Scott, KS
Helen Thomas, Ft. Scott, KS
Otie Thomas, Ft. Scott, KS
Herbert Wallace, Ft. Scott, KS
Mrs. Herbert Wallace, Ft. Scott, KS
Flo Willard, Ft. Scott, KS
Avis Alcorn, Goodland, KS
Bob Boyle, Goodland, KS
Marilyn Cooper, Goodland, KS
Dennis Daise, Goodland, KS
Elena Delarose, Goodland, KS
Bob Dull, Goodland, KS
Tina Goodwin, Goodland, KS
Wallace Hansen, Goodland, KS
Leonard Howell, Goodland, KS
Kermit Huerbert, Goodland, KS
Maxine Jacobs, Goodland, KS
Jeff Jeffreis, Goodland, KS
Al King, Goodland, KS
Clyde Lambertz, Goodland, KS
Jeff Mason, Goodland, KS
Gary McClung, Goodland, KS
Larry McClung, Goodland, KS
Mike Patterson, Goodland, KS
Clarence Scheomer, Goodland, KS
Richard Scheopner, Goodland, KS
Jason Scheopner, Goodland, KS
Van V. Vasquez, Goodland, KS
Ron Vignery, Goodland, KS
Glenda Waugh, Goodland, KS
Richard Whitman, Goodland, KS
Marlene McKay, Great Bend, KS

Mike Moore, Great Bend, KS
Tim Wiggins, Halsted, KS
Tammy "K" Schlatterbeck,
 Hamilton, KS
Marsha Anderson, Hays, KS
Tom Bahm, Hays, KS
Bernice Lundy, Hays, KS
Fred Sheesly, Hays, KS
Gunther Siems, Hays, KS
Bob Sperling, Hays, KS
Melissa Stramel, Hays, KS
Ron Stithem, Hill City, KS
Helen Bunte, Hutchinson, KS
Kirk Cottingham, Hutchinson, KS
Dan Demming, Hutchinson, KS
Sam Jones, Hutchinson, KS
Larry Tucker, Hutchinson, KS
Neva Jane Upp, Hutchinson, KS
Robert Upp, Hutchinson, KS
Mitzi Wyland, Hutchinson, KS
Chris Meyers, Iola, KS
Mitch Miller, Iola, KS
Le Ann Schaeffer, La Cross, KS
Betty Schaeffer, La Cross, KS
Dennis Schaeffer, La Cross, KS
Richard L. Ankerholz, Lyons, KS
Wendy Clark, Lyons, KS
Arnold C. Cline, Lyons, KS
Judy Jones, Lyons, KS
Audrey Krautzer, Lyons, KS
Mike Robinson, Lyons, KS
Linda Sunley, Lyons, KS
Gerald Woodard, Maize, KS
Barbara Siefker, Moran, KS
Jamie Siefker, Moran, KS
Ashley Siefker, Moran, KS
Chuck Kourieht, Natoma, KS
Bob Clark, Newton, KS
Guy Cuber, Newton, KS
Jonny Jackson, Newton, KS

Rich Cornell, Olathe, KS
Wes Robinson, Potpotwin, KS
Vickie Angell, Sabetha, KS
Scott W. Angell, Sabetha, KS
Tobe Zweygardt, St Francis, KS
Gene Medenwald, Stafford, KS
Mardell Degood, St. Francis, KS
Paul Degood, St. Francis, KS
Jannetta Evina, St. Francis, KS
Chet Gartner, St. Francis, KS
Kate Kelly Giengers, St. Francis, KS
Bruce Hefner, St. Francis, KS
Karen Krien, St. Francis, KS
George Kruse, St. Francis, KS
Esther Lauer, St. Francis, KS
Gary Lawrence, St. Francis, KS
Rev. Gary Lawrence, St. Francis, KS
Barbara Lawrence, St. Francis, KS
Christy Lawrence, St. Francis, KS
Rob Lawson, St. Francis, KS
Bob Lewis, St. Francis, KS
Glorianne Milne, St. Francis, KS
Vicky Pitmann, St. Francis, KS
Frank Schlepp, St. Francis, KS
Jessie Shiefeld, St. Francis, KS
June Stellberg, St. Francis, KS
Martha Stothard, St. Francis, KS
Betty Winston, St. Francis, KS
Ruth Ann Yonkey, St. Francis, KS
M.L. Yonkey, St. Francis, KS
Merlin Yonkey, St. Francis, KS
Tobe Zweygardt, St. Francis, KS
Fred Phelps, Topeka, KS
Darrol K. Griffith, Toronto, KS
Virginia Matthews, Tribune, KS
Kim Newman, Uniontown, KS
Ed Brungardt, Victoria, KS
Jake Barton, Wakeeney, KS
Kathy Lamb, Whitewater, KS
Mary Ann Christensen, Wichita, KS

Linda Gerber, W. Newton, KS
Sam Gerber, W. Newton, KS
Malanie Smeltzer, Edgewood, KY
Ted Osborn, Lexington, KY
Dwayne Bays, Lexington, KY
Gregory Carter, Louisa, KY
Clyde Franks, Stanford, KY
Mario Chamarro, Stockbridge, MA
Doreen Mattingly, Worchester, MA
Bessie Sadler Smith, Bowie, MA
Helen Cafferly, Brunswick, ME
Dennis P. Ferguson II, Bay City, MI
Christie Warbasse, Dearborn, MI
Glen Harrison, Detroit, MI
Randall Reed, Detroit, MI
Kevin Jackson, Detroit, MI
Jim Flemming, Highland, MI
Don Hubbard, Royal Oak, MI
Nany I. Brooks,
    West Bloomfield, MI
Mike Thomas, Bangor, ME
Jason Bryan, Bangor, ME
Alice Thomas, Bangor, ME
Joe Holland, Mankato, MN
Mary Holland, Mankato, MN
David Spepplinij, Maple Grove, MN
Bob Guentzel, Mankato, MN
Mary Guentzel, Mankato, MN
Bill Reed, St. Cloud, MN
Rob Nelson, Thompson Falls, MT
Rich Nelson, Thompson Falls, MT
Robin Nelson, Thompson Falls, MT
Bob Nelson, Thompson Falls, MT
Dianne Nelson, Thompson Falls, MT
C. Birg, Baldwin, MO
Mak D. Wells, Baldwin, MO
Dennis R. Thompson, Sr., Balto, MO
Adam Sandoval, Beaufort, MO
Natalie Sandoval, Beaufort, MO
Luke Sandoval, Beaufort, MO

Richard Sandoval, Beaufort, MO
Earlaine Sandoval, Beaufort, MO
Kenneth R. Carr, Belle, MO
Claude Elrod, Belle, MO
Lawrence Owens, Belle, MO
Norma Quens, Belle, MO
Lawrence Quens, Belle, MO
Shan Rubenhous, Belle, MO
Bessie Sadler, Belle, MO
Daren Sight, Belle, MO
Melford Speuyroy, Belle, MO
Lyndon Thenhaus, Belle, MO
Charles Gray, Bland, MO
Jim Helnry, Bland, MO
Jill Schlottog, Bland, MO
Chuck Parrott, Blue Springs, MO
Scott Schwartz, Chesterfield, MO
Helena Aumiller, l
    Clover Bottom, MO
Charlene Aumiller,
    Clover Bottom, MO
Gloria Aumiller Hohenstreet,
    Clover Bottom, MO
Kate Peters, Emminence, MO
Joy Peters, Emminence, MO
Linda Waugh, Eureka, MO
Terry Mattingly, Foristell, MO
Don Doholt, House Springs, MO
Henry Groenewoud,
    Kansas City, MO
Ralph Miller, Lawrenceville, MO
Ed Doso, Lebanon, MO
Ralph Reynolds, Linn, MO
Cathy Mauzey, Owensville, MO
Karen Montcalm, Owensville, MO
Denise Sexton, Owensville, MO
Luther Willhill, Owensville, MO
John Hawthorne, Palmyra, MO
Mary Lou Hawthorne, Palmyra, MO
Don Crandell, Poplar Bluff, MO

Kathy Knudsen, Rolla, MO
Don Farris, St. Clair, MO
Vernon Starks, St. Clair, MO
Allen L. Jones, St. James, MO
Larry F. Brott, St. Joseph, MO
Ann Friend, St. Louis, MO
Linda Kamp Waugh, St. Louis, MO
Wade Piersel, St. Peters, MO
Kieth Piersel, St. Peters, MO
Glen Ballau, Union, MO
Daniel Biermann, Union, MO
Laura Biermann, Union, MO
Harold Breeding, Union, MO
Karen Carson, Union, MO
Ron Carson, Union, MO
James Downard, Union, MO
Wayne Dreier, Union, MO
John C. Garvey, Union, MO
Marshall Heresta, Union, MO
Phillep Klemme, Union, MO
Rick A. Matthiesen, Union, MO
Bob Purschke, Union, MO
Darla Riley, Union, MO
Ken Rohrbach, Union, MO
Harold Schmidt, Union, MO
Ken Schmidt, Union, MO
Valorie Steinbeck, Union, MO
Larry Wellman, Union, MO
Berniece Westermann, Union, MO
Barabra Wisman, Union, MO
Bill Williams, Vichy, MO
Vichy Runyon, Vienna, MO
John Runyon, Vienna, MO
Ed Smith, Webster Grove, MO
Karen Smith, Webster Grove, MO
Frankie Smith, Webster Grove, MO
Bob Miller, West End, NC
Polly Miller, West End, NC
Binnert De Jong,
   Leiden, Netherlands

Peter Heemskerk,
   Leiden, Netherlands
Lucy Zengerink,
   Leiden, Netherlands
Monica Versteegh,
   Leiden, Netherlands
Joseph Pinto, Bariton, NJ
Dianne Nevitt, Basking Ridge, NJ
Alvin Hyman, Bayonne, NJ
Bob Oxfurth, Belleville, NJ
Joy A. Bard, Branchburg, NJ
Gary Goodenow, Branchburg, NJ
Dan Lacosta, Branchburg, NJ
Richard Weiner, Branchburg, NJ
Joseph Brizzi, Bridgewater, NJ
Beverley Chandler,
   Bridgewater, NJ
Bart Johnson, Bridgewater, NJ
Fran Johnson, Bridgewater, NJ
Ned Luiten, Bridgewater, NJ
Charles N. Miller, Bridgewater, NJ
Ralph Nevitt, Bridgewater, NJ
Al Salin, Clinton Tuff, NJ
Jack Regan, Far Hills, NJ
S. Dipaula, Flemington, NJ
Neil Ariano, Labertville, NJ
Bill Brown, Labertville, NJ
Joseph Gazzillo, Labertville, NJ
Jack Guillerne, Labertville, NJ
Ted Nahen, Manasquan, NJ
Richard Stockhammer, Milford, NJ
Gretchen Perera, N. Caldwell, NJ
Kevin McCoy, Piscataway, NJ
John Stella, Plainfield, NJ
Bob Oxfurth, Somerset, NJ
George Chandler, Somerville, NJ
Tim Deuitch, Somerville, NJ
Nate Falk, Somerville, NJ
John Gich, Somerville, NJ
Dick Henry, Somerville, NJ

Freas Hess, Somerville, NJ
Carl Hockenbury, Somerville, NJ
Jerry Johnson, Somerville, NJ
Peter Johnson, Somerville, NJ
John R. Seabert, Somerville, NJ
Ed Starrett, Somerville, NJ
Ron Tatro, Somerville, NJ
Bill Thompson, Somerville, NJ
Dennis Vanolst, Somerville, NJ
Lee Rochat, Sommerville, NJ
Russel Smith, Sommerville, NJ
Harold Glotzer, Sunnyside, NJ
Nelson Breining, Union, NJ
Robert Brezinsky, Union, NJ
Joe Cantalupo, Union, NJ
John J. Davis, Union, NJ
C. Richard Fried, Union, NJ
Leslie Heimall, Union, NJ
Jim Monticello, Union, NJ
Dieter Polednik, Union, NJ
Wiliam Price, Union, NJ
Evelyn Rosengarten, Union, NJ
Ken Rosengarten, Union, NJ
Lou Vecchia, Union, NJ
Mirian Szepesi, Albuquerque, NM
Diane Trump, Albuquerque, NM
Skip Moss, Clovis, NM
Erika Gerling, Beatty, NV
Virginia Johnson, Beatty, NV
Hutch ?, Goldfield, NV
Dennis Hammers, Goldfield, NV
Rich White, Goldfield, NV
Kim Forshy, Henderson, NV
Josh Forshy, Henderson, NV
Peggy Forshy, Henderson, NV
Don Aper, Las Vegas, NV
Jim Bilbray, Las Vegas, NV
Dona Cassese, Las Vegas, NV
Dr. Tom Cassese, Las Vegas, NV
Rhonda Dupre, Las Vegas, NV

Bernie Farrow, Las Vegas, NV
Vince Garth, Las Vegas, NV
Dr. Joe George, Las Vegas, NV
Rick Golightly, Las Vegas, NV
Karen , Las Vegas, NV
Sam Head, Las Vegas, NV
Robert E. James, Las Vegas, NV
Rich Newman, Las Vegas, NV
Jack Petitti, Las Vegas, NV
Chris Robertson, Las Vegas, NV
Randy Robertson, Las Vegas, NV
Chuck Schenck, Las Vegas, NV
Juan Sotomayor, Las Vegas, NV
Joe Thiriot, Las Vegas, NV
Alan Trumont, Las Vegas, NV
Michael P. Phelps, Reno, NV
Hank Beals, Tonopah, NV
Kenneth Curtis, Tonopah, NV
Bill Judkins, Batavia, NY
Chuck Taylor, Batavia, NY
Mitchell Savader, Great Neck, NY
Elana Savader, Great Neck, NY
Natalie Eigen, Hewlett, NY
Stuart Eigen, Hewlett, NY
Jonas Javna, Long Island City, NY
Joanne Billharz, New York City, NY
Robert H. Billharz,
    New York City, NY
Robert Bransch, New York City, NY
Therdal Bransch,
    New York City, NY
Murray Fox, New York City, NY
Edie Fox, New York City, NY
Tom Jewell, New York City, NY
Yannick Lelay, New York City, NY
Peter Neuhaus, New York City, NY
Chris Patrovich, New York City, NY
John Shanahan, New York City, NY
Pritam Singh Thind,
    New York City, NY

Gilberto E. Soriano,
  New York City, NY
Keith Torrie, New York City, NY
Ron Khosla, Pittsford, NY
Patt Renyal, Shaddowcliff, NY
Warren Renyal, Shaddowcliff, NY
Todd Huckabone, Syracuse, NY
Pearl Y. Hu, Tamytown, NY
Susie Stewart, Albany, OH
Dave Bradford, Amelia, OH
Janey Click, Amelia, OH
Kim Costello, Amelia, OH
Johanna Davidson, Amelia, OH
Melanie Ellsi, Amelia, OH
Jody Herdtner, Amelia, OH
Quenton Hickman, Amelia, OH
Leanna Kiser, Amelia, OH
Brad Marx, Amelia, OH
Lisa Porter, Amelia, OH
Pam Simms, Amelia, OH
Kelly Smith, Amelia, OH
Andy Sturm, Amelia, OH
Georgia Deskins, Athens, OH
Fred Deskins, Athens, OH
Joe Jagers, Athens, OH
Zella Ploghoft, Athens, OH
Milton Ploghoft, Athens, OH
Joe Cubbage, Barberton, OH
Lois Bloom, Batavia, OH
Lyle Bloom, Batavia, OH
Gary Cunningham, Batavia, OH
Tina Elliot, Batavia, OH
Daniel Hannon, Batavia, OH
Dick Lahke, Batavia, OH
Roger Gibson, Belpre, OH
Jayesh Patel, Belpre, OH
Stanley Felix, Blanchester, OH
Lloyd E. Beck, Chillicothe, OH
Dick Berlger, Chillicothe, OH
Phillis L. Blevins, Chillicothe, OH

Estill Bowling, Chillicothe, OH
Henry L. Brahe, Chillicothe, OH
Steve Burkehardt, Chillicothe, OH
Mike Cheater, Chillicothe, OH
Dave Chrestensen, Chillicothe, OH
Janet Christian, Chillicothe, OH
Jack S. Clark, Chillicothe, OH
Deanna Cockrell, Chillicothe, OH
Ken Coe, Chillicothe, OH
Fred Duve, Chillicothe, OH
Don Ellis, Chillicothe, OH
Henry Galloway, Chillicothe, OH
David Gunlock, Chillicothe, OH
Harry Hatmaker, Chillicothe, OH
Richard Himes, Chillicothe, OH
Dick Holm, Chillicothe, OH
Willard Homans, Chillicothe, OH
Jack Kellenberger, Chillicothe, OH
Paul Leach, Chillicothe, OH
Dick McCutcheon, Chillicothe, OH
Bob McNish, Chillicothe, OH
Don Mumma, Chillicothe, OH
Harry Nlock, Chillicothe, OH
James Petro, Chillicothe, OH
Steve Phillips, Chillicothe, OH
Jerry Phillips, Chillicothe, OH
Mark Pitstick, Chillicothe, OH
R.L. Reynolds, Chillicothe, OH
Jim Rucker, Chillicothe, OH
Lane Schmuchen, Chillicothe, OH
Don Seingneues, Chillicothe, OH
Floyd E. Simantel, Chillicothe, OH
Jeff Smith, Chillicothe, OH
Gerald Snyder, Chillicothe, OH
Hallis Spring, Chillicothe, OH
Charlie Strong, Chillicothe, OH
Gilbert Stultz, Chillicothe, OH
Jack Thompson, Chillicothe, OH
Ron Wagner, Chillicothe, OH
Robert Wakefield, Chillicothe, OH

Janet Weeve, Chillicothe, OH
Dick Whitney, Chillicothe, OH
Eric Wissler, Chillicothe, OH
Mark Ziegler, Chillicothe, OH
Rob Anderson, Cincinnati, OH
Michell Andrews, Cincinnati, OH
Tom Auxler, Cincinnati, OH
Ronald L. Beamen, Cincinnati, OH
Berle Bernat, Cincinnati, OH
Rick A. Bernat, Cincinnati, OH
Bob Black, Cincinnati, OH
Jim Booher, Cincinnati, OH
Bob Carlson, Cincinnati, OH
Bob Connelly, Cincinnati, OH
Larry Cramer, Cincinnati, OH
Carlos Davis, Cincinnati, OH
Edna Dean, Cincinnati, OH
Dennis Devine, Cincinnati, OH
Carolyn Dugger, Cincinnati, OH
Holly R. Eckstein, Cincinnati, OH
Earl Edwards, Cincinnati, OH
Victor Fowler, Cincinnati, OH
Nick Franceschia, Cincinnati, OH
Bob Gerethel, Cincinnati, OH
Don Grepps, Cincinnati, OH
Eric R. Grogg, Cincinnati, OH
John Hackett, Cincinnati, OH
Dale Haller, Cincinnati, OH
Fred Hill, Cincinnati, OH
Paul M. Hoffman, Cincinnati, OH
Christy Hogue, Cincinnati, OH
Charles Hutchinson, Cincinnati, OH
Christy Jacobs, Cincinnati, OH
Henry Jernigan, Cincinnati, OH
Fammy Koons, Cincinnati, OH
Charles Kron, Cincinnati, OH
Phylllis Laubisch, Cincinnati, OH
Fred Lueche, Cincinnati, OH
Shauna Lynch, Cincinnati, OH
Calvin Marcum, Cincinnati, OH

Marc A. McCartney, Cincinnati, OH
Sheila McGaughlin, Cincinnati, OH
David McNatt, Cincinnati, OH
Carla Mopper, Cincinnati, OH
Terry Munz, Cincinnati, OH
Dave O'Connor, Cincinnati, OH
Marcus Patterson, Cincinnati, OH
Dick Patterson, Cincinnati, OH
Ken Rahe, Cincinnati, OH
Ed Schrano, Cincinnati, OH
Amy Sheafer, Cincinnati, OH
Rod Sinenenes, Cincinnati, OH
Peggy Sirk, Cincinnati, OH
Judy Skeons, Cincinnati, OH
Chuck Smith, Cincinnati, OH
Bill Spreln, Cincinnati, OH
Dan Sway, Cincinnati, OH
Bill Thompson, Cincinnati, OH
Warren Tipton, Cincinnati, OH
Jim Tredway, Cincinnati, OH
Mary Trlinie, Cincinnati, OH
Robert L. Viettel, Cincinnati, OH
Larry Voss, Cincinnati, OH
Terry A. White, Cincinnati, OH
Mike Williams, Cincinnati, OH
Chief R.E. Willis, Cincinnati, OH
Richard L. Martin, Clarmont, OH
Wallace Bradford, Coolsville, OH
S. Linden Moore, Dayton, OH
Todd Gentry, Dillsboro, OH
Sheik McIntosh, Dillsboro, OH
Bill Hutier, Dublin, OH
Alan Cromberger, Fayetteville, OH
Kelly Overstree, Fayetteville, OH
John Reihle, Fayetteville, OH
Rhonda Swain, Fayetteville, OH
Mrs. Mably Corts, Fayetville, OH
Joe Miller, Fayetville, OH
Mike Robinson, Fayetville, OH
Patty Sims, Fleming, OH

Kary Snyden, Frankfort, OH
Violet M. Ham, Greenfield, OH
Juanita Murray, Greenfield, OH
Marguerite Penn, Greenfield, OH
Wayne F. Gordey, Hallsville, OH
Lorena Armintrout, Hillsboro, OH
Betty Beekman, Hillsboro, OH
Bob Beiser, Hillsboro, OH
James L. Byrd, Hillsboro, OH
Bob Conrad, Hillsboro, OH
Winfred Hakes, Hillsboro, OH
Adaline Hartman, Hillsboro, OH
Tina L. Hill, Hillsboro, OH
Barbara Kirk, Hillsboro, OH
Marcus Lewis, Hillsboro, OH
Phil McElwee, Hillsboro, OH
Anna B. Miller, Hillsboro, OH
Heber Newell, Hillsboro, OH
Caryl Newell, Hillsboro, OH
John E. Payne, Hillsboro, OH
Lydia Phillips, Hillsboro, OH
Virginia Pitstick, Hillsboro, OH
Bill Pitstick, Hillsboro, OH
Harold Pitzer, Hillsboro, OH
Charles Price, Hillsboro, OH
Norma Pucket, Hillsboro, OH
Ester Rotruff, Hillsboro, OH
Jim Williamson, Hillsboro, OH
Dorothy Gall, Leesburg, OH
Tom Gall, Leesburg, OH
Martha Walker, Leesburg, OH
Barb Patterson, Londonderry, OH
Ralph Swackhammer,
    Londonderry, OH
Bill Caitens, Loveland, OH
Nancy Olson, Loveland, OH
Joe Cowdery, Marietta, OH
Roger W. Doak, Marietta, OH
Art Edwards, Marietta, OH
Charlie Fogle, Marietta, OH

Carla Hitchcock, Marietta, OH
Nancy Hollister, Marietta, OH
Carl R. Lynch, Marietta, OH
Barbara Davis, McArthur, OH
Debbie Hill, McArthur, OH
Dora Lowe, McArthur, OH
Clarice Peck, McArthur, OH
Jim Williams, McArthur, OH
Carolyn Dugger, Milford, OH
Ellis Green, Milford, OH
Gene Gully, Milford, OH
Richard Sydnor, Milford, OH
Bob Young, Milford, OH
Charles F. Ware, New Richmond, OH
Theresa Knudsen, Rolla, OH
Kevin Karpacs, Sardis, OH
Albert Hendershot, Waterford, OH
John Hocker, Waverly, OH
Lynne Kempton, Waverly, OH
Tommy D. Thompson, Hammon, OK
Eileen Torpey, Corvallis, OR
Edgar Weimeer, Adah, PA
Harold Weimer, Adah, PA
Bruce Burns, Bedford, PA
Steve Zimmerman, Bedford, PA
Leslie Ballantyne, Buchingham, PA
John W. Phillips, Carmichael, PA
Nadine Deardorff,
    Chambersburg, PA
Peggy D Vaine, Chambersburg, PA
Emory Todd, Chester Springs, PA
Philip R. Dann, Chlog, PA
Robert Coover, Coatsville, PA
Donald Dayton, Coatsville, PA
Martin Kennedy, Coatsville, PA
Heidi Hauice, Columbia, PA
Sharon Sarver, Confluence, PA
Nan Shutt, Confluence, PA
Richard Stouffer, Connellsville, PA
Yvonne L. Duncan, Downington, PA

Charles J. Maruzzella,
Downington, PA
John Moka, Downington, PA
Deb Cook, Fairhope, PA
Rich Cook, Fairhope, PA
John Cassel, Fairview Village, PA
Darryl Hettrick, Fairview Village, PA
Christine Johnson,
Fairview Village, PA
Barry Barlup, Fayetville, PA
Karen A. Decyk, Ft. Loudon, PA
John W. Decyk II, Ft. Loudon, PA
William J. Decyk II, Ft. Loudon, PA
William J. Decyk III, Ft. Loudon, PA
Jacques Family Rest., Gap, PA
Helen Family Rest., Gap, PA
Rich Fenton, Gettysburg, PA
James R. Graham, Gettysburg, PA
Christopher Koontz, Gettysburg, PA
Ervedt Krafa, Jr., Gettysburg, PA
Pierre Lutt, Gettysburg, PA
Barbara Burkholder, Hagerstown, PA
David Burkholder, Hagerstown, PA
Bob Conrad, Hanover, PA
Mike Hufnagle, Hanover, PA
Tom Hufnagle, Jr., Hanover, PA
Jim Frem, Harrisburg, PA
Doris Roberts, Harrisburg, PA
Jim Roberts, Harrisburg, PA
Cee Stopper, Harrisburg, PA
Troy Herring, Hellam, PA
Travis Phillips, Holbrook, PA
Carol J. Phillips, Holbrook, PA
Gerald E. Phillips, Jr., Holbrook, PA
Gerald E. Phillips, Sr., Holbrook, PA
Harry B. Burns, Hopewell, PA
Joseph M. Kluska, Jr., Hopwood, PA
John Fetper, Intercoarse, PA
Rebecca Bloodsworth, Jacobus, PA
David Epps, Kimberton, PA

Susan Grear, Kimberton, PA
Andy Grear, Kimberton, PA
Dick Grear, Kimberton, PA
Robert Raichle, Kimberton, PA
Kerry Knepper, Kingwood, PA
Gayle Knepper, Kingwood, PA
Mike Trimpny, Kirkwood, PA
Sally Rankin, Knob Fork, PA
Chris Rankin, Knob Fork, PA
Don Rankin, Knob Fork, PA
Charles L. Roberts, Knob Fork, PA
Helen M. Dommel, Lancaster, PA
Donna Evans, Lancaster, PA
Andrea Miller, Lancaster, PA
Dick Ocho, Lancaster, PA
Vit L. Patel, Lancaster, PA
Carl Stresclul, Lancaster, PA
Hugh K. Urey III, Lancaster, PA
Kathleen Warner, Lancaster, PA
Chris Stancey, Lansdale, PA
Helena Sheldon, Malvern, PA
Vernon Shire, Sr., Manheim, PA
Joly Marietta, Marklesburg, PA
Gayle Knepper, Markleton, PA
Kerry Knepper, Markleton, PA
John McCahill, McClellandtown, PA
Nelson Keperliy, Mountville, PA
Dorothy Kline, New Castle, PA
Cherish Brown, New Centerville, PA
Philip Beckett, New Hope, PA
Thomas Fitzpatrick, New Hope, PA
Philip Toy, New Hope, PA
Judith Toy, New Hope, PA
Gary E. Reed, New Oxford, PA
Richard Grossman, Parkesburg, PA
Adam Grossman, Parkesburg, PA
Cindy Grossman, Parkesburg, PA
Deb Grossman, Parkesburg, PA
Amanda Grossman, Parkesburg, PA
Tom Grossman, Parkesburg, PA

Nabila Makram, Parkesburg, PA
Joyce Bustard, Phoenixville, PA
Richard Grear, Phoenixville, PA
Susan Grear, Phoenixville, PA
Robin Levin, Phoenixville, PA
Ronald Petrou, Phoenixville, PA
Julia Raab, Pittsburg, PA
Skip Miller, Pomerey, PA
Daniel Cramer, Rockwood, PA
Barry Ray, Rockwood, PA
Bill Doman, Ronks, PA
Jody Corearo, Scranton, PA
Kevin Keating, Shrewsbury, PA
Betty Livery, Somerset, PA
Mark Miller, Somerset, PA
Pam Miller, Somerset, PA
Mark V. Burchfield,
    Thomasville, PA
Matthew V. Coble, Thomasville, PA
Dan Harrow, Trent, PA
Bryan Rose, Warminster, PA
Debbie Hill, Waynesburg, PA
Travis Walls, Waynesburg, PA
Tom Walls, Waynesburg, PA
Janet Walls, Waynesburg, PA
Linda Keller, Waynsboro, PA
John Keller, Waynsboro, PA
Dawn Bowlen, Waynsburg, PA
Pat Headley, Waynsburg, PA
Claire-Jean Bardolf, York, PA
Lereva Barnhart, York, PA
Jil Berrymann, York, PA
Delores J. Clewell, York, PA
Ray Jackson, York, PA
Chris Jackson, York, PA
Joe Lepley, York, PA
Ed Lincoln, York, PA
Christina E. Patton, York, PA
Greg Rice, York, PA
Douglas Shaffer, York, PA

Linda Shire, York, PA
Vernon H. Shire, Jr., York, PA
Bill Slothowen, York, PA
Earl P. Thomas, York, PA
Sarah Thomas, York, PA
Gerald E. Shoemaker, York Co, PA
Jett Villegar, Manila, Phil
Boby Rutierrez, Manila, Phil
Ivy Marquez, Manila, Phil
Vicky Fillarca, Manila, Phil
Fritz Tenny, Lyssuch, Switzerland
Reuben S. Hunter, Knoxville, TN
Reuben A. Hunter, Knoxville, TN
Mark Johnstone, Austin, TX
Bob Richter, Bellaire, TX
Madie Richter, Bellaire, TX
Oliver Mattingly, Dallas, TX
Walter Brown, Garland, TX
Janice Peairson, Houston, TX
Dawn Perkins, Houston, TX
Susan Christian, Houston, TX
Libby Whitmire, Houston, TX
Zachary ?, , USA
Bob Nalwalker, Circleville, UT
Jenny Sorensen,
    Dameron Valley, UT
Richard Berg, Junction, UT
Sue Berg, Junction, UT
Lynda Norton, Junction, UT
Sandy Youne, Junction, UT
Collin Campbell, Laverkin, UT
Steve Hall, Laverkin, UT
Robert Hill, Laverkin, UT
Migan Hill, Laverkin, UT
Tacy Hill, Laverkin, UT
Jet Hirschi, Laverkin, UT
Daniel Pelley, Laverkin, UT
Andrew Pelley, Laverkin, UT
Beverlee Shamo, Laverkin, UT
David Ostler, Layton, UT

Anita Sanders, Salina, UT
Mack Austin, Springdale, UT
Mike Goudey, Springdale, UT
Logan Hebner, Springdale, UT
Brad Quinn, Springdale, UT
Jack Tibus, Springdale, UT
Anne Augustine, St George, UT
Becky Fackrell, St George, UT
Royce Jones, St George, UT
Miriam Self, St George, UT
Larry Johnson, Virgin, UT
Robert L. Stropky, Bothell, WA
Shelly Sheaman, Moses Lake, WA
Kieth Sheaman, Moses Lake, WA
Kenneth S. Fetterman, Renton, WA
Sara Lewis, Wenatche, WA
Summer Angard, Wenatchee, WA
Sara Lewis, Wenatchee, WA
Sharon Lang, Marshfiels, WI
David Bayer, Milwankee, WI
Matt Bayer, Milwankee, WI
Paul Schmidt, Milwankee, WI
Tony Howe, Portage, WI
Dave Howe, Portage, WI
August Stellberg, Beloit, WI
Stella Rose, Alma, WV
Gordon Rose, Alma, WV
Iris Bale, New Martinsville, WV
Mary Bissett,
    New Martinsville, WV
Bill Boggs, New Martinsville, WV
Iris C. Bokr, New Martinsville, WV
Wooddy Broadwater,
    New Martinsville, WV
Vern Hunt, New Martinsville, WV
Jan Cooker Kearns,
    New Martinsville, WV
Bob J. Keffer, New Martinsville, WV
Alex Moles, New Martinsville, WV

Stacey L. Moles,
    New Martinsville, WV
Norman Morris,
    New Martinsville, WV
Rick Morris, New Martinsville, WV
Bill Parish, New Martinsville, WV
Helen Powell, New Martinsville, WV
Jim Quinet, New Martinsville, WV
R.K. Sersitling,
    New Martinsville, WV
Clyde Smith, New Martinsville, WV
Dean Stutler, New Martinsville, WV
Sharron Winer,
    New Martinsville, WV
Sam Winer, New Martinsville, WV
Vicki L. Gallagher, Paden City, WV
Tressa Goots, Paden City, WV
John Wm. Goots, Sr.,
    Paden City, WV
C.R. Huff, Paden City, WV
Helen D. Marn, Paden City, WV
Barbara Pusinger, Paden City, WV
Eric Cutright, Pennsboro, WV
Bonnie Brown, Reder, WV
Dave Mikes, Sistersville, WV
Bill Butterfield, St. Marys, WV
Chris Gironton, St. Marys, WV
Randa Hall, St. Marys, WV
Tammy Hammett, St. Marys, WV
Bill Hammett, St. Marys, WV
Jim McCeddrick, St. Marys, WV
Durlus Nicholson, St. Marys, WV
Oroz Polino, St. Marys, WV
Bob Pryor, St. Marys, WV
Mike Reese, St. Marys, WV
J.R. Sinton, St. Marys, WV
Brenda Tucker, St. Marys, WV
Maynard D. Grant, Cheyenne, WY
Mark Squillace, Laramie, WY

Here's how to order additional copies of

The Long Walk Home
by Matt Mattingly

Please send $12.95 per copy + $4.00 shipping for 1st copy; add $1.00 shipping for each additional copy to the same address. Books are shipped by 1st class mail. California orders: Please add 7.25% sales tax per book ($.94) for all orders shipped to California addresses.

Your Name (please print) _____

Address to send book(s) _____

_____

No. of copies ordered_____   Amount enclosed _____

Please make checks payable to Sonora Used Books
and mail checks to

Sonora Used Books
21 S. Washington Street
Sonora, CA 95370